ALWAYS HUNGRY!

Library and Archives Canada Cataloguing in Publication

Title: Always hungry! / Laurent Dagenais ; photographs by Renaud Robert and William Langlais.

Other titles: Toujours faim! English

Names: Dagenais, Laurent, author. | Robert, Renaud (Photographer), photographer. | Langlais, William, photographer.

Description: Translation of: Toujours faim! | Includes index.

Identifiers: Canadiana 2023014666X | ISBN 9780778807148 (hardcover)

Subjects: LCSH: Cooking. | LCGFT: Cookbooks.

Classification: LCC TX714 .D32513 2023 | DDC 641.5—dc23

Design: Brian Finn

Layout and production: PageWave Graphics Inc.

Editor: Michelle Meade

Proofreader: Judy Phillips

Indexer: Gillian Watts

Cover Photography: Renaud Robert and William Langlais

Interior Photography: Renaud Robert and William Langlais except for:

        pages 16, 17, 154–159, 224 (courtesy of Laurent Dagenais)

        pages 2, 18–23, 204–205, 207 (courtesy of Unsplash)

Food Styling: Laurent Dagenais

We acknowledge the support of the Government of Canada.

Canadä

Published by Robert Rose Inc.

120 Eglinton Avenue East, Suite 800, Toronto, Ontario, Canada M4P 1E2

Tel: (416) 322-6552 Fax: (416) 322-6936

www.robertrose.ca

Printed and bound in China

3 4 5 6 7 8 9 ESP 31 30 29 28 27 26 25 24

ALWAYS HUNGRY!

Laurent Dagenais

PHOTOGRAPHS BY
RENAUD ROBERT AND WILLIAM LANGLAIS

TABLE OF CONTENTS

INTRODUCTION

I have always believed that fate takes us where we need to go. I often remind myself of this at times of uncertainty in my personal and professional life. Sitting at my computer writing a cookbook is definitely proof that fate has more than one trick up its sleeve. Seeing how my life has totally changed since I created video content is like science fiction for me. We always say these things only happen to other people — until they happen to us. Although I never show this side of myself in my videos, I am constantly battling impostor syndrome…

When I first started cooking, I was always the first person to joke about celebrity chefs. For me, the only way to be a "real" chef meant working as part of a kitchen team, being on the front lines, in the trenches, working 15 hours a day for starvation wages. Why? To become head chef is rare but a complete validation. Do I still think you have to experience this process to become a "real" chef or cook? 100%. But I also believe it's important to do what you love. I hope I can encourage others to follow their passions wherever that may lead them… into a kitchen or in front of a camera!

Cooking has made me a better person. I don't know where I would be today if I hadn't been encouraged to take a cooking course ten years ago. I never liked school, and my grade-point average was living proof! I spent a year at a CEGEP (a junior college in Quebec) in a program that interested me less than my smoke breaks in the park, so I dropped out. Working in the local skateboard shop sounded like a lot more fun… Until my parents told me I had to pay rent if I wasn't in school. That was a shock.

After a few years of navigating the culinary world, including a stint in Whistler, British Columbia, I lost the desire to work in a professional kitchen. I then turned to "the dark side": catering! For a few months, my life took me behind a bar (as you'll see here in this book). When I returned to Montreal, I managed the opening of a new restaurant and then worked my way up: general manager of another restaurant, partner and director of operations for two others… It was during this time that I started making my food videos. They helped me keep my passion for cooking alive and well!

When the pandemic hit and restaurants and bars had to close, I started creating more and more content. Even on a small scale (at the time), I saw that the handful of people who followed me seemed to really like my recipes and how I presented them. My girlfriend, Amandine, did the filming. She eventually convinced me to set up a TikTok account to broadcast them. Hmm… I hesitated, thinking that this app was just for teens and that all you would find there were dance videos of dubious taste. After posting one of our first videos, which went viral overnight, I realized the incredible potential of this platform. A few months later, I left my job, my financial stability, my insurance and all the benefits that came with that life to dedicate myself full-time to this new adventure.

Many people encouraged me; others tried to talk me out of taking this risk. Today, I can say that this leap into the unknown was the best decision I've ever made. As I said, the videos are one way to fire up my passion for cooking. I can now share this love with more than a million subscribers around the world and make my living from it.

The book you are holding in your hands is not meant to show you the latest cooking trends or ground-breaking techniques used in the restaurants with the most Michelin stars in the world. It reflects what you can see in my many videos on social media: unpretentious food, the promotion of quality ingredients treated with respect and the use of basic techniques done properly. This book is also an opportunity to share with you some bits of my life and some anecdotes related (or not) to the world of food – and it is a gentle reminder to everyone that cooking is sharing, cooking is love, cooking is friendship and, above all, cooking is pleasure.

I'll say it again: fate takes us where we need to go! If this book makes you want to cook, I will have achieved my goal. And I secretly hope that my recipes will always make you hungry…

I was hungry.

Still hungry…

CHAPTER 1

CONDIMENTS

PRESERVED LEMONS

INGREDIENTS

15 lemons

1 cup (250 ml) coarse salt no. 8

1/2 cup (125 ml) granulated sugar

1 tbsp (15 ml) black peppercorns (optional)

Lemon juice (enough to cover the lemons)

An indispensable part of Maghrebi cuisine, this condiment is mainly used to add intense lemon flavors to couscous dishes and tagines without the tartness found in regular lemons. It is easy to make, but the flavors are complex. Salt, sugar, acid and time will turn a simple lemon into an explosion of flavors.

MAKES	PREP TIME	PICKLING TIME
2 x quart (1 L) Mason jars	30 minutes	6 weeks

Wash lemons, make a few cuts in the skin and squeeze; collect juice. Set juice aside.

In a bowl, combine lemons, coarse salt, sugar and peppercorns (if using), making sure the seasonings get right into the cuts.

Divide lemons between two 1-quart (1 L) Mason jars and cover them with the juice. Pack the lemons well in the jars so they are completely covered with liquid. If needed, add filtered water to cover. Refrigerate for at least 6 weeks.

Once opened, preserved lemons can be stored in the fridge for up to 6 months.

MARINATED BIQUINHO PEPPERS

INGREDIENTS

1/2 cup (125 ml) biquinho peppers or your preferred chile

2 garlic cloves

1 tsp (5 ml) black peppercorns (optional)

3 tbsp (45 ml) granulated sugar

3 tbsp (45 ml) salt

1 cup (250 ml) white vinegar

These little teardrop-shaped peppers, also called "devil's tears," are from Brazil. Surprisingly, they aren't very spicy. Their potency can vary depending on the soil and climate where they grow. They are crunchy and juicy, with a slight citrus taste and a smoky finish — like their distant cousin the habanero. Once marinated, not only will these peppers keep very well in the fridge, but their flavor will be enhanced. It's the perfect condiment to wow the crowd at your next cocktail party!

MAKES	PREP TIME	COOKING TIME
2 cups (500 ml)	5 minutes	5 minutes

Put peppers in a pint-sized (475 ml) Mason jar.

In a small saucepan, combine garlic, peppercorns (if using), sugar, salt and vinegar. Add 1 cup (250 ml) water and bring to a boil over medium heat. Pour mixture over biquinho peppers. Let cool completely. Keep in the Mason jar in the fridge.

Once opened, the peppers can be stored in the fridge for up to 6 months.

MAPLE-MARINATED MUSTARD SEEDS

INGREDIENTS

8 coriander seeds

6 black peppercorns (optional)

2 cloves

3/4 cup (175 ml) mustard seeds

2 bay leaves

Pinch salt

1 1/4 cups (310 ml) white wine vinegar + extra to taste

1/2 cup (125 ml) maple syrup + extra to taste

If you want to impress your guests the next time you have people over, add maple-marinated mustard seeds to a beet salad or charcuterie board. For extra points, tell them it's mustard caviar!

MAKES	PREP TIME	COOKING TIME
4 cups (1 L)	5 minutes	10 minutes

In a small skillet, dry roast (without any added fat) coriander seeds, peppercorns (if using), and cloves over medium-low heat until fragrant. Transfer spices to a small saucepan.

Add the remaining ingredients and 1/2 cup (125 ml) water. Bring to a boil over medium-high heat.

Reduce heat to medium-low and simmer for 10 minutes. Remove the saucepan from the heat and let cool to room temperature.

Season to taste with more vinegar and/or maple syrup. Transfer to a sterilized jar and store in the fridge. The mixture can become too thick after a few days or weeks because the mustard seeds have absorbed all the liquid. If needed, add 1 tbsp (15 ml) vinegar to thin it out and you're good to go!

Once opened, the mustard seeds can be stored in the fridge for up to 6 months.

MARINATED WILD LEEKS

INGREDIENTS

1 lb (500 g) wild leeks (ramps)

4 cups (1 L) white vinegar

1 1/4 cups (310 ml) granulated sugar

Pinch salt

1 tbsp (15 ml) black peppercorns (optional)

2 sprigs fresh thyme

Ahhh, wild leeks! Prized by chefs, wild leeks (also known as ramps) are not available everywhere — in Quebec, for example, they have been designated as a vulnerable species since 1995 and cannot be sold. Only harvesting in small amounts is permitted. Wild leeks have a short growing season, so the best way to be able to enjoy this product is to marinate it. You can use the marinated wild leek bulbs like capers in your dishes and add the marinade to your salad dressings.

MAKES	PREP TIME	COOKING TIME	MARINATING TIME
2 x quart (1 L) Mason jars	10 minutes	5 minutes	1 week

Divide the wild leeks into two quart (1 L) Mason jars.

In a saucepan, combine vinegar, sugar and salt. Bring to a boil over medium-high heat. Pour the hot vinegar over the wild leeks. Add peppercorns (if using) and thyme. Refrigerate for about 1 week.

Once opened, the wild leeks can be stored in the fridge for up to 6 months.

DILL PICKLES

INGREDIENTS

6 or 7 Kirby cucumbers

MARINADE

1 to 2 large garlic cloves

1 to 2 bay leaves (optional)

2 cups (500 ml) white vinegar

5 tbsp (75 ml) salt

1 tbsp (15 ml) black peppercorns

1 tbsp (15 ml) coriander seeds

1/4 tsp (1 ml) calcium chloride
(such as Bernardin Pickle Crisp)

Pinch mustard seeds

1 bunch fresh dill

Pickles are one of the most popular condiments in North America and Europe. When I was little, my dad taught me (thanks, Pops) that, if you go to Schwartz's Deli in Montreal, you order the smoked meat sandwich with fries, a black cherry Cott's soda and a pickle. That's it. If you don't have a jar of pickles in your fridge, now's your chance.

MAKES	PREP TIME	PICKLING TIME
2 x quart (1 L) Mason jars	2 days	1 month

Day 1. Wash cucumbers, then soak them in a bowl of ice water for 30 minutes. Drain, then put them in the fridge.

Combine all marinade ingredients except dill in a medium saucepan. Add 2 cups (500 ml) water and bring to a boil. Remove from heat and let cool. Refrigerate.

Day 2. Divide cucumbers into two 1-quart (1 L) Mason jars. Pour cold marinade over pickles and add dill. Refrigerate for 1 month.

Once opened, cucumbers can be stored in the fridge for up to 6 months.

GRILLED PINEAPPLE SALSA VERDE

INGREDIENTS

6 tomatillos

4 to 6 jalapeño peppers

2 sweet banana peppers

2 poblano peppers

2 green onions

1 white onion, cut into 1-inch (2.5 cm)-thick rings

1/2 pineapple, peeled and cored

Salt

6 tbsp (90 ml) avocado oil, divided

5 garlic cloves

1 bunch fresh cilantro

1 avocado, peeled and coarsely chopped

1 tsp (5 ml) ancho chile powder

1 tsp (5 ml) guajillo chile powder

1 tsp (5 ml) chipotle chile powder

1 tsp (5 ml) ground annatto seeds

1 tsp (5 ml) ground coriander

1 tsp (5 ml) ground cumin

1 tsp (5 ml) ground oregano

Juice of 3 limes

3 or 4 ice cubes

Freshly ground black pepper

This salsa is amazing! The jarred salsa you get from the grocery store is only good for nachos. If you want to be the taco master at your next Mexican fiesta, put a bowl of grilled pineapple salsa verde on the table and you're golden!

MAKES	PREP TIME	COOKING TIME
About 4 cups (1 L)	20 minutes	6 minutes

Preheat a grill or skill over high heat.

Place tomatillos, peppers, green onions, onion and pineapple on a large baking sheet and salt generously. Add 2 tbsp (30 ml) avocado oil and mix well.

Add mixture to the hot grill or skillet and grill for 2 to 3 minutes on each side, until nicely grilled.

Transfer vegetables to a blender or food processor. Add garlic, cilantro, avocado, spices, salt to taste, lime juice, the remaining 4 tbsp (60 ml) avocado oil and ice cubes. Mix until smooth. Season to taste with salt and pepper.

TROPICAL SALSA

INGREDIENTS

2 tomatoes, finely diced

1 red onion, diced

1 mango, peeled and finely diced

1 banana pepper, seeded and diced

1 habanero pepper, seeded and diced

1 poblano pepper, seeded and diced

1/2 bunch fresh cilantro, finely chopped

Juice and zest of 2 or 3 limes

3 tbsp (45 ml) avocado oil

1 1/2 tsp (7 ml) ground cumin

1 tbsp (15 ml) tajine seasoning

Salt

The first time I made this salsa was for a video featuring shrimp tacos on a beach in Sayulita, on the west coast of Mexico. I'm pretty confident when I cook for other people, but the diners were Mexican this time and there was a lot of pressure. Luckily, once I saw their smiles and high fives, I knew the mission was accomplished.

MAKES	PREP TIME
About 4 cups (1 L)	20 minutes

In a bowl, mix all ingredients except salt. Season to taste with salt. Refrigerate.

BBQ SAUCE

INGREDIENTS

5 cups (1.25 L) tomato sauce

1 cup (250 ml) honey

1 cup (250 ml) cider vinegar

3/4 cup (175 ml) molasses

1 1/2 tsp (7 ml) salt

1 tsp (5 ml) garlic powder

1 tsp (5 ml) Aleppo pepper

1/4 tsp (1 ml) chili powder

1/4 tsp (1 ml) hot sauce

A few drops of Worcestershire sauce

To take your ribs or pulled pork to the next level, this is the sauce you want!

MAKES	PREP TIME	COOKING TIME
about 4 cups (1 L)	5 minutes	10 to 15 minutes

In a saucepan, bring all ingredients to a boil over medium heat. Reduce heat to medium-low and cook for 10 to 15 minutes, until the mixture is reduced by half and has thickened to your desired consistency.

BBQ sauce can be stored in an airtight container in the fridge for 1 week.

ZA'ATAR OIL

INGREDIENTS

1 tbsp (15 ml) ground sumac

1 tbsp (15 ml) ground cumin

1 tbsp (15 ml) dried thyme

1 tbsp (15 ml) toasted sesame seeds

1 tsp (5 ml) salt

1 tsp (5 ml) freshly ground black pepper

2 cups (500 ml) vegetable oil

We are hearing the word "za'atar" more and more often when it comes to cooking, but no one really knows what it is! Za'atar is the name of a family of herbs, but it's also the name of a spice blend that includes these herbs, toasted sesame seeds and sumac. I like to make an oil with it because the mixture stays fresh longer. It's the perfect condiment to brush over grilled vegetables or to add to a vinaigrette or an herbed yogurt. Use it on all your favorite meats and vegetables!

MAKES	PREP TIME	COOKING TIME
About 4 cups (1 L)	5 minutes	5 minutes

Place all ingredients except oil in a glass or heatproof container.

Heat oil in a saucepan to 150°F (65°C). Carefully and slowly pour it over the other ingredients. Let cool, then keep in the fridge in a sealed container.

The oil can be stored in the fridge for up to 1 year.

CHAPTER 2

SOUPS

CUCUMBER GAZPACHO

INGREDIENTS

8 Persian cucumbers or 2 English cucumbers, coarsely chopped

2 cups (500 ml) buttermilk

12 drops jalapeño hot sauce (green Tabasco)

Salt and freshly ground black pepper

Extra virgin olive oil, for drizzling

GARNISHES

1/4 cup (60 ml) sour cream

A few sprigs of fresh dill

The perfect recipe to start summer off on the right foot! Serve it as is or add chunks of cucumber and feta cheese, along with pickled red onions.

SERVINGS	PREP TIME	REFRIGERATION TIME
4	15 minutes	1 hour

In a blender, combine cucumbers, buttermilk, hot sauce, salt and pepper and blend until smooth.

Add a drizzle of olive oil.

Strain gazpacho through a sieve and into a bowl. Refrigerate for at least 1 hour.

Serve very cold in chilled bowls and drizzle with olive oil. Garnish each bowl with 1 tbsp (15 ml) sour cream and a sprig of dill.

ALL-DRESSED CREAM OF POTATO SOUP

CREAM SOUP

2 tbsp (30 ml) olive oil

2/3 cup (150 ml) butter

5 to 6 garlic cloves, peeled and crushed

1 Spanish onion, cut into 1-inch (2.5 cm)-thick rings

1 leek (white and light green parts only), washed and cut into 1-inch (2.5 cm)-thick rings

Salt and freshly ground black pepper

5 Yukon Gold potatoes, peeled and cut into 1-inch (2.5 cm)-thick slices

10 cups (2.5 L) vegetable stock

2 to 3 sprigs fresh thyme

2 to 3 sprigs fresh rosemary

1 1/4 cups (310 ml) heavy or whipping 35% cream

FOR SERVING

1 large loaf of round rustic bread

10 strips cooked smoked bacon, diced or crumbled

1 cup (250 ml) grated white Cheddar cheese

1 cup (250 ml) sour cream

5 to 6 green onions, finely sliced

Freshly ground black pepper

This is the most comforting soup ever! The bread bowl isn't a new idea, but it's always a winner. It's like eating a giant all-dressed baked potato, with the bread replacing the potato skin.

MAKES	PREP TIME	COOKING TIME	RESTING TIME
About 16 cups (4 L)	40 minutes	1 hour 10 minutes	10 minutes

Heat olive oil and butter in a large saucepan over medium heat, until butter is melted. Add garlic, onion and leek. Season with salt and pepper. Cover, then reduce heat to medium-low. Sauté for 10 to 12 minutes, until vegetables are translucent. Stir every 3 to 4 minutes to prevent them from browning.

Add potatoes and sauté for 3 or 4 minutes. Pour in stock and bring to a simmer.

Tie a piece of string around the sprigs of thyme and rosemary to create a bouquet garni. Add it to the soup.

Cook over low heat for 30 to 40 minutes, until the potatoes are tender. Let cool for 5 to 10 minutes.

Squeeze the bouquet garni to the last drop into the soup, then throw it away. Stir in cream. Using a hand blender, blend until smooth. Season with salt and pepper. Keep warm.

Preheat oven to 400°F (200°C).

With a bread knife, cut off the top of the loaf. Using a spoon or your hands, scoop out the inside to make a bread bowl. Toast bread bowl in the oven for 8 to 10 minutes. (The leftover bread can be used to mop up the delicious soup or made into croutons.)

Ladle hot soup into the bread bowl. Garnish with bacon, cheese, sour cream, green onions and a good crack of pepper.

MAPLE PARSNIP SOUP

INGREDIENTS

2 tbsp (30 ml) olive oil

2 tbsp (30 ml) butter

12 parsnips, peeled

4 to 5 garlic cloves, peeled and crushed

1 onion, sliced

1 leek (white and light green parts only), cut into rings

2 sprigs fresh thyme, leaves chopped + extra for garnish

2 sprigs fresh rosemary, leaves chopped

3 tbsp (45 ml) maple syrup

3/4 cup (175 ml) white wine

4 cups (1 L) vegetable stock

1 cup (250 ml) heavy or whipping 35% cream

Extra virgin olive oil, for drizzling

CROUTONS

1 tbsp (15 ml) olive oil

1 tbsp (15 ml) butter

2 garlic cloves, peeled and crushed

1 sprig fresh thyme

1/2 baguette, cut into 1-inch (2.5 cm) cubes

The combination of parsnip and maple is just incredible. I can't tell you why, but it's legendary. Period.

SERVINGS	PREP TIME	COOKING TIME
4 to 6	20 minutes	45 minutes

Heat olive oil and butter in a large saucepan over high heat. Add parsnips and cook for 6 to 8 minutes, until nicely caramelized. Reduce heat to medium, then add garlic, onion and leek and cook for 10 minutes, or until onion is softened and translucent. Add thyme and rosemary.

Pour in maple syrup, then deglaze with wine and cook until it is completely reduced. Add stock, bring to a boil and cook for 20 to 25 minutes, until parsnips are cooked. Stir in cream and simmer for 2 minutes.

Transfer soup to a food processor and pulse until smooth. Return soup to the saucepan and keep warm.

For the croutons: Meanwhile, heat and butter in a skillet over medium-high heat. Add garlic, thyme and bread cubes and cook for 5 to 6 minutes, until crusty and golden. Stir often to prevent croutons from burning.

Ladle into individual bowls. Garnish soup with croutons and a sprig of thyme and drizzle extra virgin olive oil on top.

CAULIFLOWER AND SWEET POTATO SOUP WITH HARISSA

INGREDIENTS

2 tbsp (30 ml) olive oil

2 tbsp (30 ml) butter

1 red onion, diced

4 garlic cloves, finely chopped

2 tbsp (30 ml) smoked paprika

1 1/2 tbsp (22 ml) ground cumin

1 1/2 tsp (7 ml) ground coriander

1 tsp (5 ml) fennel seeds, crushed

1 to 2 tbsp (15 to 30 ml) harissa, depending on your desired spiciness

1 large cauliflower, cut into florets

3 sweet potatoes, peeled and diced into 1/2-inch (1 cm) cubes

1 cup (250 ml) cooked chickpeas, drained

1/2 cup (125 ml) marinated roasted red peppers, diced

2 cups (500 ml) crushed or diced tomatoes

5 cups (1.25 L) vegetable stock

4 cups (1 L) packed fresh baby spinach (about 4 oz/125 g)

Salt and freshly ground black pepper

The mild flavor of the cauliflower combines with the sweetness of sweet potatoes and harissa spice — this soup is off the charts!

SERVINGS	PREP TIME	COOKING TIME
4 to 6	10 minutes	30 minutes

Heat oil and butter in a large saucepan over medium-high heat. Add onion and sauté for 4 to 5 minutes. Add garlic, paprika, cumin, coriander, fennel seeds and harissa. Cook for 2 to 3 minutes, stirring frequently to prevent the spices from burning.

Add cauliflower, sweet potatoes, chickpeas and roasted red peppers. Mix well and cook for 2 to 3 minutes.

Add tomatoes and stock. Bring to a boil, then reduce heat to low. Cook for 15 to 20 minutes, until cauliflower and sweet potatoes are tender when pierced with a sharp knife.

Add spinach and cook for another 2 to 3 minutes. Season with salt and pepper.

Ladle soup into bowls and garnish with 1 tbsp (15 ml) yogurt, sesame seeds, cashews, cilantro leaves and lemon zest. Drizzle olive oil on top and add a small dollop of harissa.

GARNISHES

4 to 6 tbsp (60 to 90 ml) Greek
yogurt

1 tsp (5 ml) toasted black sesame
seeds

1 tsp (5 ml) toasted white sesame
seeds

2 tbsp (30 ml) toasted cashews

1 tbsp (15 ml) fresh cilantro
leaves

1 tsp (5 ml) lemon zest

Extra virgin olive oil, for
drizzling

Harissa

POZOLE

SERVINGS	PREP TIME	COOKING TIME
8 to 10	40 minutes	2 hours

INGREDIENTS

1 3/4 lb (875 g) pork shoulder

1 large white onion, diced, divided

4 garlic cloves, chopped, divided

2 tbsp (30 ml) chili powder

1 tbsp (15 ml) ground cumin

1 tbsp (15 ml) fresh oregano

1 tsp (5 ml) freshly ground black pepper

2 tbsp (30 ml) avocado oil or canola oil

1 bunch fresh cilantro, chopped with stems and leaves separated

4 cups (1 L) corn kernels

3 cups (750 ml) pork stock

2 poblano peppers, grilled

1 jalapeño pepper, diced

GARNISHES

3 ancho peppers + extra for garnish

1 garlic clove

4 to 5 limes, cut into wedges

4 to 5 radishes, sliced

A few fresh cilantro sprigs

1 small green cabbage, thinly sliced

Tortilla chips

Place pork shoulder in a saucepan, cover with water and add a generous pinch of salt. Slowly bring to a boil over medium heat, then reduce heat to low. Using a small ladle or a spoon, skim off any scum from the surface.

Add half the onion, three-quarters of the garlic, chili powder, cumin, oregano and pepper. Cook over low heat for 45 minutes. Carefully transfer pork shoulder to a plate and set aside.

Heat oil in another saucepan over medium-high heat. Add the remaining onion (set aside 2 tbsp/30 ml for garnish), remaining garlic and cilantro stems. Sauté for 5 to 6 minutes, until onion is translucent.

Meanwhile, cut pork shoulder into 1-inch (2.5 cm) cubes and add to the saucepan. Stir.

Add corn, stock (top up with chicken stock or water if needed) and peppers. Bring to a boil over medium heat, then reduce heat to low. Cover and simmer for 45 to 60 minutes, until meat, onion and peppers are very tender.

For the garnish: Bring 4 cups (1 L) water to a boil in a small saucepan. Add ancho peppers and boil over medium-high heat for 15 minutes, until peppers are tender.

In a blender or food processor, combine 1 1/2 cups (375 ml) water, drained ancho peppers, garlic and the 2 tbsp (30 ml) of reserved onion. Mix for a few seconds. Pour into a bowl or gravy boat and place it in the center of the table so people can serve themselves.

Using a small ladle or serving spoon, skim off any fat from the surface of the soup and discard. Ladle soup into bowls. Garnish with ancho peppers, lime, radishes, cilantro, cabbage and tortilla chips.

CHAPTER 3

SALADS

GREEN PAPAYA SALAD

SALAD

2 shallots, finely chopped

1 green papaya, peeled and cut into thin matchsticks

1 carrot, peeled and cut into thin matchsticks

1 small bunch fresh cilantro, chopped

1 bunch fresh Thai basil, chopped

1 x (3-oz/85 g) package beef jerky, cut into thin matchsticks

CHILE VINAIGRETTE

1 to 2 bird's eye chiles, finely sliced

1/4 cup (60 ml) roasted peanuts

2 tbsp (30 ml) palm sugar

2/3 cup (150 ml) light soy sauce

Juice of 3 limes

Salt

GARNISHES

1/4 cup (60 ml) roasted peanuts

A few fresh cilantro leaves

Thai basil leaves (optional)

Lime wedges (optional)

My relationship with green papaya salad goes back to my trip to Thailand in 2016. That was the first time I really explored the world of spices. My friend Frank and I gave ourselves the challenge of ordering dishes that were as spicy as the locals were eating. It didn't take us long to order the popular green papaya salad. After one bite, our mouths were instantly on fire and we were sweating! A nice cold beer helped calm the heat and we suddenly felt cooler. It seems counterintuitive, but eating really spicy food in a hot country is apparently one way to cool off. I spent a long time developing this recipe, which draws on my favorite ingredients from the Thai and Vietnamese versions of this salad.

SERVINGS	PREP TIME
4	25 minutes

For the salad: In a large bowl, mix all ingredients.

For the chile vinaigrette: In a bowl or jar, vigorously mix all vinaigrette ingredients. Season to taste with more salt.

Pour vinaigrette over salad and toss. Transfer to a large plate, garnish with peanuts and cilantro. Add basil leaves and lime wedges (if using) and serve.

TOMATO, CORN, SNOW PEA AND RICOTTA SALAD

SERVINGS	PREP TIME	COOKING TIME
2 to 4	30 minutes	6 minutes

SALAD

1 cup (250 ml) ricotta

2 tbsp (30 ml) extra virgin olive oil + extra for drizzling

Juice of 1 lemon

Fleur de sel

1 loaf bread or baguette, cut into 1-inch (2.5 cm)-thick slices

4 or 5 heirloom tomatoes, cut into wedges

1 cup (250 ml) cooked sweet corn kernels or 1 to 2 cobs of cooked corn, kernels shaven off

10 snow peas, trimmed and thinly sliced

A few basil leaves

HONEY VINAIGRETTE

1 tbsp (15 ml) chopped pickled garlic scapes or garlic cloves

1 tsp (5 ml) honey

Dash balsamic vinegar

Pinch hot pepper flakes

1/2 cup (125 ml) extra virgin olive oil

Salt and freshly ground black pepper

For the salad: In a bowl, combine ricotta, olive oil, lemon juice and a pinch of fleur de sel and mix until ricotta is fluffy, smooth and creamy.

Preheat a barbecue or broiler. Drizzle bread with oil and season with fleur de sel on both sides. Grill sliced bread until crusty. Cut into croutons.

For the honey vinaigrette: In a bowl, combine all ingredients and mix well.

Spread ricotta in a shallow dish. Arrange tomatoes, corn and snow peas on top. Drizzle with vinaigrette, then garnish with basil and croutons.

NIÇOISE SALAD

SERVINGS	PREP TIME	COOKING TIME
2 to 4	30 minutes	25 to 35 minutes

LEMON VINAIGRETTE

2 tbsp (30 ml) freshly squeezed lemon juice

2 tsp (10 ml) Dijon mustard

1/4 tsp (1 ml) salt

1/4 tsp (1 ml) freshly ground black pepper

6 tbsp (90 ml) extra virgin olive oil

NIÇOISE SALAD

2 large eggs

Salt and freshly ground black pepper

3 oz (90 g) bluefin tuna

6 to 8 fingerling potatoes

3 garlic cloves, peeled and crushed

1 sprig fresh thyme

Extra virgin olive oil, for drizzling

12 green or yellow beans, trimmed

2 Persian cucumbers, diced

1 small vine tomato, diced

1 shallot, chopped

1/2 cup (125 ml) Niçoise olives, pitted and cut in half

For the vinaigrette: In a large bowl, whisk lemon juice, mustard, salt and pepper. Gradually add oil, whisking until vinaigrette is smooth and emulsified. Season to taste with salt and pepper.

For the salad: Put eggs into a small saucepan and cover them with cold water. Bring to a rolling boil over high heat. Turn off the heat and cook for 7 minutes. When cool enough to handle, peel and cut into wedges. Set aside.

Bring 8 cups (2 L) water to a boil in a medium saucepan. Add a small pinch of salt. Place tuna in a spider strainer or slotted spoon and plunge it into the water for 20 seconds, or until outer part of fish turns opaque gray. Transfer immediately into a large bowl of ice water to stop the cooking. (This tataki technique, which is very popular in Japan, ensures a more uniform exterior cooking than when tuna is seared in a skillet.) Remove tuna from the ice water and pat dry with a paper towel. With a sharp knife, cut tuna into 1-inch (2.5 cm)-thick slices.

Refrigerate until it's time to serve.

Slowly bring 4 cups (1 L) cold water to a boil in a small saucepan. Add potatoes, garlic, thyme and a generous pinch of salt. Reduce heat to low and cook for 20 to 25 minutes, until potatoes are tender. Drain, then transfer to a baking sheet. Drizzle oil over potatoes and let cool completely at room temperature. Cut in half lengthwise and set aside.

Bring a small saucepan of water to a boil. Add beans and blanch for 2 to 3 minutes. Drain, then plunge them into a bowl of ice water to stop the cooking. Drain and set aside.

In a large bowl, combine potatoes, beans, cucumbers, tomato, shallot and olives. Add a little lemon vinaigrette, salt and pepper and toss. Season to taste with more vinaigrette if needed.

Transfer salad to a large serving platter. Top with slices of tuna and egg wedges. Drizzle with vinaigrette.

COLD MUSSEL SALAD

MUSSELS

1 lb (500 g) mussels

Extra virgin olive oil, for drizzling

Hot sauce, for drizzling (optional)

A few sprigs of fennel fronds

Fresh bread, to serve

MARINATED FENNEL

1/4 cup (60 ml) granulated sugar

Pinch salt

3/4 cup + 1 tbsp (190 ml) white vinegar

1/2 cup (125 ml) thinly sliced fennel

TOMATO VINAIGRETTE

1 tomato, cut into large chunks

3 tbsp (45 ml) extra virgin olive oil

2 tbsp (30 ml) fennel vinegar

Hot sauce, as desired

Salt and freshly ground black pepper

This classic seafood salad is delicious on a warm summer's day. Fresh mussels are perked up with marinated fennel and a tomato vinaigrette. This salad may look soupy, but that's alright! The vinaigrette is made with very little oil, so we can add it more generously.

SERVINGS	PREP TIME	COOKING TIME
2 to 4	30 minutes	10 minutes

For the mussels: Rinse mussels and debeard them. Add 1 cup (250 ml) water to a large skillet. Bring to a boil, add mussels and cover. Steam mussels for 5 to 7 minutes, until they open. Remove mussels from shells (discarding shells) and refrigerate.

For the marinated fennel: In a saucepan, combine sugar, salt and vinegar. Bring to a boil over medium-high heat. Remove from heat and add fennel to the saucepan. Let cool.

For the vinaigrette: In a blender, pulse all vinaigrette ingredients until smooth. Season to taste with more salt and pepper. Strain and refrigerate.

When serving, pour vinaigrette into a shallow serving dish. Drizzle with oil and hot sauce (if using) and arrange mussels on top of vinaigrette. Garnish with marinated fennel and fennel fronds. Serve with fresh bread.

NORTHERN SHRIMP SALAD WITH ASPARAGUS GAZPACHO

GAZPACHO

2 green onions, green part only

1 Persian cucumber, coarsely chopped

1/2 bunch blanched asparagus, coarsely chopped, and tips reserved for salad

1/2 bunch fresh mint, leaves only

1/2 bunch fresh parsley

1/2 bunch fresh dill

1/2 cup (125 ml) extra virgin olive oil

3 tbsp (45 ml) Wild Leek vinegar (page 33) + extra to taste

Juice of 1 lemon + extra to taste

1 to 2 ice cubes

Salt and freshly ground black pepper

The end of spring brings with it the promise of hot summer days, but it's also my favorite time of year thanks to the arrival of incredible products, including northern shrimp and early asparagus. This salad is an explosion of freshness in your mouth. As you eat it, you will feel like you're sitting on a beach with your toes in the sand!

SERVINGS	PREP TIME	COOKING TIME
2	15 minutes	4 to 5 minutes

For the gazpacho: Put all ingredients in a blender or food processor and mix until smooth. To keep gazpacho green and cold, add ice cubes while pulsing. Season to taste, adding more vinegar or lemon juice as needed. Refrigerate.

For the shrimp salad: In a small bowl, mix all ingredients.

Ladle gazpacho into two chilled shallow plates or bowls. Top with shrimp salad. Dollop sour cream on top, drizzle with oil and garnish with lemon zest.

SHRIMP SALAD

3 1/2 oz (100 g) northern shrimp, shelled and cooked

1/2 cup (125 ml) fresh or frozen peas, blanched in salted water

Reserved asparagus tips

2 tsp (10 ml) extra virgin olive oil

Salt and freshly ground black pepper

GARNISHES

2 tbsp (30 ml) sour cream

2 tsp (10 ml) extra virgin olive oil

Lemon zest

GRILLED ZUCCHINI AND CARROT SALAD WITH ZA'ATAR VINAIGRETTE

ZA'ATAR VINAIGRETTE

Zest and juice of 1/2 lemon

3 tbsp (45 ml) Za'atar Oil (page 42)

2 tsp (10 ml) Dijon mustard

2 tsp (10 ml) maple syrup

GRILLED ZUCCHINI AND CARROT SALAD

2 yellow zucchini

2 green zucchini

1 tbsp (15 ml) salt

Extra virgin olive oil, for drizzling

4 rainbow carrots, peeled

Freshly ground black pepper

Seeds (arils) from 1/4 pomegranate

3 tbsp (45 ml) pistachios, finely chopped

1 cup (250 ml) crumbled feta cheese (about 5 oz/150 g)

1/4 bunch fresh cilantro, leaves only

SERVINGS	PREP TIME	COOKING TIME
2 to 4	25 minutes	25 to 35 minutes

For the vinaigrette: Combine all ingredients in a small Mason jar and shake vigorously until mixture is smooth.

For the salad: Cut the zucchini in half lengthwise and, with the tip of a small knife, make small cuts in the flesh.

Place zucchini in a large colander, sprinkle with salt and let drain for 20 minutes. Pat dry with a paper towel, place on a baking sheet and drizzle with olive oil. Set aside.

Preheat barbecue to medium-high. Drizzle oil over carrots, season with salt and pepper and place them on the upper grill. Grill for 20 minutes, turning them regularly for uniform cooking. When carrots are nearly done (check by inserting the tip of a small knife into largest carrot), season zucchini with pepper. Place zucchini on lower grill and grill each side for 3 minutes, or until grill marks appear. Cut zucchini into triangles.

Arrange carrots and zucchini in a large shallow serving dish, alternating as you go. Pour some vinaigrette over the grilled vegetables and garnish with pomegranate seeds (arils), pistachios, feta and cilantro.

SUCRINE SALAD WITH DILL RANCH DRESSING

DILL RANCH DRESSING

1/3 cup (75 ml) mayonnaise

1/3 cup (75 ml) buttermilk

1/3 cup (75 ml) sour cream

1 to 2 garlic cloves, finely chopped

1/2 bunch fresh dill, chopped

2 tbsp fresh parsley, chopped

1 tbsp (15 ml) freshly squeezed lemon juice + extra to taste

1 tsp (5 ml) cider vinegar

Zest of 1 lemon

Salt and freshly ground black pepper

SUCRINE SALAD

15 green beans, blanched

5 to 7 thin red onion slices

4 to 5 radishes, thinly sliced

3 or 4 heads sucrine or baby romaine lettuce, leaves separated, washed and spun

2 Persian cucumbers, thinly sliced

1/4 fennel bulb, thinly sliced using a mandoline

1/2 bunch fresh tarragon, leaves only

1/4 cup (60 ml) sunflower seeds

The only time you'll see me put ranch dressing on a salad is when it's homemade ranch. Time to pitch the ancient bottle in your fridge and make the real thing.

SERVINGS	PREP TIME	COOKING TIME
2	15 minutes	4 to 5 minutes

For the dill ranch dressing: In a small bowl, whisk mayonnaise, buttermilk and sour cream until smooth. Add the remaining ingredients and whisk again. Refrigerate.

For the salad: In a large bowl, combine all ingredients. Add enough dressing to coat sucrine or baby romaine leaves. Season to taste with salt, pepper or lemon juice.

Transfer to a large serving bowl and toss to give lettuce leaves extra volume.

CHAPTER 4
SANDWICHES

SPICY PORK MEATBALL BANH MI

CARROT AND DAIKON RADISH SALAD

2 carrots, peeled and cut into thin matchsticks

1 cup (250 ml) daikon radish, peeled and cut into thin matchsticks

2 tbsp (30 ml) cane sugar or granulated sugar

1/2 tsp (2 ml) salt

3 tbsp (45 ml) rice vinegar

2 tsp (10 ml) sesame oil

The flavors of this Vietnamese sandwich are as complex as its history. Banh mi *means "wheat bread," a derivative of the French term* pain de mie, *meaning "sandwich bread." With this recipe, I did something I thought was impossible: get my girlfriend to eat cilantro! I think she's even starting to like it…*

SERVINGS	PREP TIME	REFRIGERATION TIME	COOKING TIME
4	1 hour 10 minutes	1 hour 20 minutes	10 minutes

For the carrot and daikon radish salad: In a large bowl, mix all ingredients. Refrigerate for 1 hour, tossing salad occasionally.

For the spicy pork meatballs: Line a baking sheet with parchment paper and set aside.

In a bowl, combine all ingredients except oil. With your hands, make 20 meatballs, about 1 inch (2.5 cm) in diameter, and place them on the prepared baking sheet. Put in the freezer for 20 minutes to chill. (This will facilitate cooking.)

Heat oil in a large nonstick skillet over medium-high heat. Cook meatballs for 8 minutes, until they are cooked through and all sides are nicely browned.

For the assembly: In a small bowl, combine mayonnaise and Sriracha. Spread mixture on the insides of the baguettes. Fill sandwich with salad, meatballs, jalapeño, if desired, and cilantro.

SPICY PORK MEATBALLS

1 lb (500 g) ground pork

3 garlic cloves, chopped

1 green onion, chopped

2 tbsp (30 ml) fresh cilantro, chopped

2 tbsp (30 ml) fresh Thai basil, chopped

1 tbsp (15 ml) cornstarch

2 tsp (10 ml) cane sugar or granulated sugar

1 tbsp (15 ml) fish sauce (nam pla)

1 tbsp (15 ml) Sriracha or sambal oelek

Salt and freshly ground black pepper

1 tbsp (15 ml) vegetable oil

ASSEMBLY

1/4 cup (60 ml) mayonnaise

2 tsp (10 ml) Sriracha

1 baguette, cut in 4 equal parts and lightly toasted

1 jalapeño pepper, thinly sliced (optional)

1/2 bunch fresh cilantro

MEXICAN TORTA WITH EGGS AND CHORIZO

INGREDIENTS

2 tbsp (30 ml) vegetable oil, divided

1 lb (500 g) Mexican chorizo sausage, casings removed

6 large eggs

Salt and freshly ground black pepper

1 1/2 cups (375 ml) refried pinto beans

6 bolillo rolls, small baguettes or ciabattas, cut in half lengthwise

3/4 cup (175 ml) Mexican crema or sour cream

5 oz (150 g) fresh Mexican cheese *(cotija)*, thinly sliced, or crumbled feta

1/2 red onion, diced

1/2 bunch fresh cilantro

Marinated jalapeño slices (optional)

Salsa (optional)

The morning after a night of partying in the incredible city of Yelapa, I tasted this very popular Mexican breakfast for the first time. Eating some fatty chorizo sausage with runny egg yolk was the only way to get back on my feet... so I could have a good siesta afterward.

SERVINGS	PREP TIME	COOKING TIME
6	10 minutes	20 minutes

Heat 1 tbsp (15 ml) oil in a large skillet over medium-high heat. Add chorizo and sauté for 7 minutes, or until fully cooked. Use the end of a wooden spoon to break up any larger pieces. Set aside.

Meanwhile, heat the remaining 1 tbsp (15 ml) oil in a large nonstick skillet over medium-high heat. Fry eggs, sunny side up or over easy, to the desired doneness.

Season to taste with salt and pepper.

In a small saucepan, warm refried pinto beans over medium heat.

Heat a skillet over medium heat, then add the rolls, cut side down, and grill until nicely browned. (Alternatively, toast them on a baking sheet in a 400°F/200°C preheated oven.)

Spread the insides of the rolls with Mexican crema. Add a few spoonfuls of refried pinto beans, chorizo and a few slices of cheese. Top with a fried egg, then garnish with red onion and cilantro. Serve with marinated jalapeños and salsa, if desired.

CRAYFISH ROLLS

INGREDIENTS

1 lb (500 g) crayfish meat, cooked

1 celery stalk, diced

1/2 red pepper, diced

1 tbsp (15 ml) capers, finely chopped

2 tbsp (30 ml) mayonnaise

2 tsp (10 ml) Dijon mustard

Juice and zest of 1 lemon

Salt and freshly ground black pepper

4 hot dog buns

2 tbsp (30 ml) butter, softened

1/2 iceberg lettuce, shredded

Lemon wedges (optional)

One day while I was looking for inspiration at the fish market, a huge tank filled with live crayfish caught my eye. I had the idea of making crayfish rolls. Often associated with southern US cooking, these freshwater crustaceans that look like small lobsters are definitely worth eating, despite all the shelling involved.

SERVINGS	PREP TIME	COOKING TIME
4	10 minutes	3 minutes

In a medium-sized bowl, combine crayfish, celery, red pepper and capers.

In a small bowl, combine mayonnaise and Dijon mustard, then stir in the crayfish mixture. Add lemon juice and lemon zest. Season to taste with salt and pepper.

Preheat a broiler over high heat. Put hot dog buns, open side up, on a baking sheet and open buns slightly to expose the insides. Broil until golden brown. Remove from oven and lightly butter the insides of the buns.

Place a generous spoonful of the crayfish mixture into buns and top with lettuce. Serve with a few lemon wedges (if using).

FLANK STEAK AND ONION SANDWICH

INGREDIENTS

1 lb (500 g) flank or skirt steak

2 tbsp (30 ml) butter

2 tbsp (30 ml) olive oil, divided

3/4 cup (175 ml) maple syrup

2 large Spanish onions, peeled and cut into 3/4-inch (2 cm)-thick rings

1/2 cup (125 ml) balsamic vinegar

1 sprig fresh thyme

Fleur de sel and freshly ground black pepper

1 large ciabatta loaf

3/4 cup (175 ml) mayonnaise

1/4 cup (60 ml) whole grain mustard

2 cups (500 ml) packed baby spinach (about 2 oz/60 g)

SERVINGS	PREP TIME	COOKING TIME
4	10 minutes	1 hour

Remove steak from the fridge and sit at room temperature for 5 minutes. Cover steak with plastic wrap or parchment paper. Using a small saucepan, pound it until tenderized and flattened.

In a large nonstick skillet, combine butter, 1 tbsp (15 ml) olive oil and maple syrup. Heat over medium heat until butter has melted. Add onions and sauté for 5 minutes.

Add vinegar and thyme, then cover and reduce heat to low. Cook for 35 to 40 minutes, until onions are nicely caramelized.

Preheat oven to 230°F (110°C).

Generously season steak with fleur de sel and pepper. Heat 1 tbsp (15 ml) oil in a large skillet over medium-high heat. Add steak and sear for 3 minutes on each side for medium-rare (145°F/63°C) or until cooked to your preferred doneness. Transfer meat to a plate and set aside to rest for 4 to 5 minutes. Thinly slice steak about 1/2 inch (1 cm) thick.

Meanwhile, warm ciabatta in the oven for 5 to 7 minutes.

In a small bowl, combine mayonnaise and mustard. Slice warm ciabatta in half lengthwise and liberally spread the two halves with the mayo-mustard sauce. Add spinach to the lower half, then cover with slices of steak and caramelized onions. Finish with a pinch of fleur de sel, pepper and a drizzle of oil. Close the sandwich and cut into servings.

MORELS ON TOAST

INGREDIENTS

3 1/2 oz (100 g) fresh morels (about 1 cup/250 ml)

2 tbsp (30 ml) butter, divided

Extra virgin olive oil, for drizzling

1 shallot, chopped

Salt and freshly ground black pepper

2/3 cup (150 ml) oxidized white wine (such as Savagnin or Vin Jaune from the Jura region), divided

1/2 cup (125 ml) brown veal or chicken stock

1/4 cup (60 ml) heavy or whipping 35% cream

1 thick slice bread, cut in half

1/2 bunch fresh chives, chopped

Chive flowers (optional)

What can I say about morels… I love eating them, but the hours spent trying to gather them leave a bitter taste in my mouth. Every year, I go searching for mushrooms, full of hope, and I always come back empty-handed. Luckily, we can find them, fresh or dried, fairly easily at the market or grocery store all year long!

SERVINGS	PREP TIME	COOKING TIME
2	15 minutes	15 minutes

Rinse morels with water. Plunge them in boiling water for 30 seconds, then dry them on a clean tea towel.

Heat 1 tbsp (15 ml) butter and a drizzle of oil in a skillet over medium heat. Add morels and shallot. Season to taste with salt and pepper. Cook morels for 5 minutes, or until nicely browned.

Add half the wine to deglaze skillet and simmer for 4 to 5 minutes, until completely reduced. Add stock and cook for another 4 to 5 minutes, until reduced by half. Stir in cream. Reduce to a thick consistency.

Take skillet off the heat. Stir in the remaining wine and 1 tbsp (15 ml) butter.

Toast bread, put it on plates and cover with morel sauce. Garnish with chives and chive flowers (if using). Season with salt and pepper. Enjoy with the rest of the wine!

MONTECRISTO

INGREDIENTS

3 tbsp (45 ml) mayonnaise

1 tbsp (15 ml) whole grain mustard

1 loaf white bread

1 cup (250 ml) finely grated Gruyère cheese, divided + extra to serve

1 cup (250 ml) finely grated Emmental cheese, divided

10 oz (300 g) old-fashioned ham, divided

3 large eggs

1/2 cup (125 ml) whole milk

5 tbsp (75 ml) butter, divided

A good drizzle of maple syrup (the real stuff!)

Freshly ground black pepper

The first time I tasted this legendary sandwich was at Au Pied de Cochon, a restaurant in the heart of Montreal. I counted seven different types of meat, a heavenly cheese mixture and way too much syrup for one plate. This sandwich is the ultimate combination of sweet and salty. Here is a simpler version (your liver will thank me!).

SERVINGS	PREP TIME	COOKING TIME
4 to 6	20 minutes	15 minutes

In a small bowl, combine mayonnaise and mustard.

Using a bread knife or a sharpened chef's knife, trim crust from all sides of bread loaf. Shape bread into a perfect rectangle. Cut bread lengthwise into 3 equal slices.

Spread 3 tbsp (45 ml) of the mustard mayo on 3 bread slices.

To assemble the sandwich, place half the cheese and half the ham on one slice of bread. Cover with a second slice of bread, mustard-mayo side down, and spread the top with the remaining 1 tbsp (15 ml) mustard mayo. Add the remaining cheese and ham and top sandwich with the remaining slice of bread.

Crack eggs into a rectangular dish that is large enough to hold sandwich. Whisk until smooth, then add milk.

Dip sandwich in the egg-milk mixture on all sides for several minutes so bread can absorb it.

In a nonstick skillet, melt 2 1/2 tbsp (37 ml) butter over medium heat. Add sandwich and grill on all sides until it forms a nice golden crust. Use a spatula to move sandwich often to prevent it from burning. Once butter turns brown, add more butter.

Transfer sandwich to a cutting board. Cut sandwich into 4 to 6 slices and garnish with a generous amount of maple syrup. Top with grated Gruyère and pepper.

CHAPTER 5

VEGETABLES

ASPARAGUS WITH WILD LEEK GRIBICHE

SERVINGS	PREP TIME	COOKING TIME
4	10 minutes	10 minutes

INGREDIENTS

6 large eggs

1 tbsp (15 ml) white vinegar

1 tbsp (15 ml) Dijon mustard

1/4 cup (60 ml) Wild Leek vinegar (page 33)

Salt and freshly ground black pepper

3/4 cup (175 ml) canola oil

1 shallot, chopped

A handful of fresh parsley, chopped

A handful of fresh tarragon, chopped

2 tbsp (30 ml) capers, rinsed and coarsely chopped

2 tbsp (30 ml) Marinated Wild Leeks (page 33), chopped

2 bunches asparagus

Place whole eggs in a saucepan and cover with cold water. Add white vinegar and bring to a boil over medium-high heat. Reduce heat to medium and simmer for 4 minutes. Drain, then place eggs in a bowl of ice water, stirring eggs to stop the cooking.

Peel eggs. Separate yolks from whites. Set whites aside. Place egg yolks in a tall and narrow container, such as a glass measuring cup, then add mustard, wild leek vinegar and 1/4 cup (60 ml) water. Season to taste with salt and pepper. Using a hand blender, blend to emulsify. Drizzle the oil into the mixture and continue to blend.

Refrigerate mayonnaise.

Chop egg whites and put them into a bowl. Add shallot, parsley, tarragon, capers, marinated wild leeks and the mayonnaise. Mix well. Set gribiche aside.

Cook asparagus for 2 minutes in boiling salted water. Drain, then serve with gribiche.

TOMATO AND MOZZARELLA ARANCINI

INGREDIENTS

3 tbsp (45 ml) olive oil, divided

1 shallot, finely chopped

2 to 3 garlic cloves, finely chopped

Salt and freshly ground black pepper

1 cup (250 ml) Carnaroli or Arborio rice

2/3 cup (150 ml) white wine

4 cups (1 L) hot vegetable stock

2/3 cup (150 ml) tomato sauce

2/3 cup (150 ml) grated Parmesan (about 2 oz/60 g)

2 tbsp (30 ml) butter

12 basil leaves

12 mini bocconcini

1 3/4 cups (425 ml) all-purpose flour

4 large eggs, beaten

3 cups (750 ml) bread crumbs

8 cups (2 L) canola oil

MAKES	PREP TIME	FREEZING TIME	COOKING TIME
10 to 12 arancini	40 minutes	20 minutes	40 minutes

Heat 2 tbsp (30 ml) olive oil in a skillet over medium heat. Add shallot and garlic and sauté for 2 to 3 minutes, until shallot is translucent. Season with salt and pepper.

Add rice and sauté for 4 to 5 minutes, until translucent. Add wine and reduce completely while stirring continuously.

Pour in stock, 1 cup (250 ml) at a time, letting it reduce completely and stirring continuously between each addition. Cook for 20 to 25 minutes, until rice is al dente.

Add tomato sauce, Parmesan, butter and the remaining 1 tbsp (15 ml) olive oil. Cover and cook for 2 to 3 minutes. Mix well, then transfer mixture to a baking sheet and let cool.

Using a spoon, spoon a little rice into the palm of your hand. Place a basil leaf and a mini bocconcini in the center, then close the rice around the filling and shape into a ball the size of a golf ball. Place on another baking sheet. Make the other risotto balls the same way. Freeze for 20 minutes.

To coat risotto balls, prepare three bowls: one with flour, one with beaten eggs and one with bread crumbs. Roll each of the balls in flour (shake to remove the excess), then in beaten eggs and finally in bread crumbs. Make sure balls are well covered so cheese doesn't run out in the deep fryer.

Heat canola oil in a deep fryer to 350°F (180°C).

Carefully lower arancini into oil using a slotted spoon and deep-fry for 1 to 2 minutes, until golden and crispy.

Transfer to a platter, sprinkle with salt and serve right away.

LOBSTER MUSHROOM RISOTTO

INGREDIENTS

2 tbsp olive oil, divided + extra for drizzling

6 oz (175 g) lobster mushrooms, chanterelles or porcini, sliced

Salt and freshly ground black pepper

2 shallots, finely chopped

2 to 3 garlic cloves, finely chopped

1 cup (250 ml) Carnaroli or Arborio rice

1 cup (250 ml) white wine

4 cups (1 L) hot vegetable stock

2 tbsp (30 ml) butter + extra as needed

1 cup (250 ml) grated Parmesan + extra as needed (about 3 oz/90 g)

4 to 5 parsley leaves

For those who haven't seen the documentary Fantastic Fungi *on Netflix, here's a fun fact: the lobster mushroom* (Hypomyces lactifluorum)*, despite its common name, is not a mushroom but a parasite that grows on certain species of mushrooms. It gets its name from its orangey-red color, which resembles the shell of a cooked lobster.*

SERVINGS	PREP TIME	COOKING TIME
2 to 4	20 minutes	40 minutes

Heat 1 tbsp (15 ml) oil in a skillet over high heat. Add mushrooms and sauté for 5 to 6 minutes. Season with salt and pepper. Transfer to a plate and set aside.

Heat the remaining 1 tbsp (15 ml) oil in the same skillet over medium-high heat. Add shallots and garlic and sauté for 3 to 4 minutes, until translucent but not browned. Add rice and sauté for 4 to 5 minutes. Season with salt and pepper, then deglaze with wine. Stir continuously for 4 to 5 minutes, until wine has almost completely evaporated.

Add stock, 1 cup (250 ml) at a time, and let the liquid evaporate almost completely between each addition, stirring continuously.

When the rice is almost al dente, add mushrooms and any remaining stock. Cook for 3 minutes, or until rice is al dente.

Add butter and cheese, cover and let rest for 2 to 3 minutes.

With a spoon, stir risotto until nice and creamy. Add more butter or cheese if needed — the more the better!

Serve in a bowl or on a plate, drizzle oil on top and garnish with parsley. It doesn't hurt to sprinkle more cheese on top!

GRENOBLE-STYLE CAULIFLOWER

INGREDIENTS

7 oz (210 g) bacon slices

3 tbsp (45 ml) butter

1 medium cauliflower, separated into florets (about 8 cups/800 g)

Salt and freshly ground black pepper

1 lemon, divided into segments and diced (see Note)

2 tbsp (30 ml) capers

1 cup (250 ml) fresh chopped parsley

GARNISH

1/2 cup (125 ml) store-bought fried onions

Legend has it that this popular garnish in French cuisine, which originated in the city of Grenoble, came to be when local chefs wanted to mask the strong taste of some fish of questionable freshness… This delicious garnish will enhance your favorite fish and vegetable dishes!

SERVINGS	PREP TIME	COOKING TIME
4 to 6	20 minutes	25 minutes

Preheat oven to 375°F (190°C).

Place bacon on a baking sheet and bake for 15 minutes. Transfer bacon to a plate and reserve fat. Set bacon aside to cool, then chop.

Heat a large skillet over medium-high heat. Add butter and bacon fat. Once butter starts to brown, add cauliflower, salt and pepper. Cook for 10 minutes, or until cauliflower is nicely toasted and tender.

Add bacon, diced lemon, capers and parsley and mix well. Transfer to a plate, garnish with fried onions and serve.

Note: To segment a citrus, use a sharp paring knife to trim off the top and bottom. Hold the citrus upright and carefully slice off the peel, following the shape of the fruit. Remove as much of the white pith as possible. Hold the fruit in your palm and carefully make two cuts inside the membrane walls to cut out the segment. Rotate the citrus and repeat until all segments have been removed.

RAPINI WITH ANCHOVIES

INGREDIENTS

1/2 cup (125 ml) olive oil

1/4 cup (60 ml) minced garlic

2 tsp (10 ml) chili flakes

2 tbsp (30 ml) freshly squeezed lemon juice

2 tbsp (30 ml) anchovies (preferably white), coarsely chopped

1 bunch rapini

1/3 cup (75 ml) grated Parmesan

SERVINGS	PREP TIME	COOKING TIME
4 to 6	20 minutes	5 minutes

Heat oil in a skillet over medium heat. Add garlic and lightly sauté for 2 minutes, until golden. Add chili flakes, then stir in lemon juice. Add anchovies and set aside at room temperature.

Bring a saucepan of salted water to a boil. Add rapini and blanch for 3 minutes. Drain, then transfer to a serving plate. Top with the anchovies and sprinkle with Parmesan.

CREAMY UDON NOODLES WITH MUSHROOMS

INGREDIENTS

14 oz (400 g) fresh or frozen udon noodles

1 tbsp (15 ml) vegetable oil

6 cremini mushrooms, thinly sliced

8 shiitake mushrooms, thinly sliced

5 oz (150 g) shimeji or enoki mushrooms

1/4 cup (60 ml) butter

2 tbsp (30 ml) light soy sauce

1 green onion, white parts chopped and green parts cut into thin strips

4 garlic cloves, chopped

1/4 cup (60 ml) dashi (or chicken or vegetable stock)

1/2 cup (125 ml) heavy or whipping 35% cream

Salt and freshly ground black pepper

SERVINGS	PREP TIME	COOKING TIME
2	10 minutes	15 minutes

If using frozen udon noodles, place them in a bowl and soak in hot water until the noodles separate. Drain and set aside.

Heat oil in a large skillet over high heat. Add mushrooms and sauté for 5 minutes, or until lightly browned and liquid has nearly evaporated. Add the butter, soy sauce, the white part of the green onion and garlic. Cook for 2 to 3 minutes.

Add dashi and bring to a simmer. Stir in cream. Add udon and cook for another 2 to 3 minutes to thicken the sauce, stirring to keep the noodles from sticking. Season to taste with salt and pepper.

Transfer the mixture to a large, shallow serving dish and garnish with the green onion strips.

SWEET POTATO AND BLACK BEAN TOSTADAS

INGREDIENTS

1/4 cup (60 ml) avocado oil + extra for greasing and drizzling

8 corn tortillas

2 large sweet potatoes

1 tsp (5 ml) smoked paprika

1 tsp (5 ml) ground cumin

1 tsp (5 ml) chili powder

1 tsp (5 ml) garlic powder

Salt and freshly ground black pepper

1 x (14-oz/398 ml) can black beans

GARNISHES

2 avocados, peeled and diced

2 radishes, thinly sliced

8 oz (250 g) Mexican fresh cheese (*queso fresco*), crumbled

3/4 cup (175 ml) Mexican crema or sour cream

1/2 red onion, diced

1/2 bunch fresh cilantro, leaves only

Salsa, as desired

SERVINGS	PREP TIME	COOKING TIME
4	15 minutes	55 minutes

Preheat oven to 400°F (200°C).

Using a brush or your hands, grease one or two large baking sheets. Place tortillas on the greased baking sheet(s) in a single layer and brush them with 1/4 cup (60 ml) oil. Salt lightly. Bake for 5 minutes, turn tortillas over and cook for another 5 minutes, or until crispy as a chip. Remove from oven and let cool. Set aside.

Increase oven temperature to 425°F (220°C). Line a small baking sheet with parchment paper or foil.

With a fork, prick sweet potatoes all over and place them on the prepared baking sheet. Bake for 45 minutes, or until the tip of a sharp knife can be easily inserted into the middle of a sweet potato.

Remove from the oven and let cool for a few minutes.

Cut sweet potatoes in half. Using a spoon, scoop flesh into a bowl and mash with a fork. Season with smoked paprika, cumin, chili powder and garlic powder. Season to taste with salt and pepper.

Combine black beans, a little water and a drizzle of oil in a small saucepan. Cook over low heat for 3 minutes, until heated through. Season with salt and pepper.

Assemble tostadas by topping tortillas with sweet potatoes and black beans. Garnish with avocado, radishes, fresh cheese, Mexican crema, onion and cilantro. Serve with salsa.

CHAPTER 6

FISH

FRIED COD WITH SWEET CHILI SAUCE

SERVINGS	PREP TIME	COOKING TIME
2	30 minutes	15 minutes

SWEET CHILI SAUCE

1 cup (250 ml) white vinegar

1 cup (250 ml) granulated sugar

1 tbsp (25 ml) sambal oelek

1 thick slice gingerroot

1 small carrot, finely grated

FRIED COD

1/4 cup (60 ml) buttermilk

1 cup (250 ml) egg whites

1 1/4 cups (310 ml) all-purpose flour, divided

1 cup (250 ml) cornstarch

8 oz (250 g) cod or other white fish

Canola oil, enough for frying

Salt and freshly ground black pepper

1 tsp (5 ml) dried seaweed (nori), dulse or flaked sea lettuce

For the sweet chili sauce: In a saucepan, combine all ingredients except carrot. Heat over low heat for 5 to 7 minutes, until syrupy and reduced by half. Discard gingerroot. Take the pan off the heat, then stir in carrot. Set aside.

For the fried cod: In a bowl, whisk buttermilk and egg whites. To another bowl, add 1/4 cup (60 ml) flour. In a third bowl, mix the remaining 1 cup (250 ml) flour and cornstarch.

Heat oil in a large skillet to 350°F (180°C). Cut fish into strips. Bread fish by dipping it first in flour, then in the egg white mixture and finally in the flour-cornstarch mixture. Using a spider strainer or slotted spoon, gently lower fish into the oil and fry for about 4 minutes.

Place the fried fish on paper towels to drain. Season with salt, pepper and dried seaweed.

Serve with sweet chili sauce.

HALIBUT WITH AMANDINE SAUCE

INGREDIENTS

2 x (5 oz/150 g) pieces halibut with skin on

Salt and freshly ground black pepper

1/4 cup (60 ml) olive oil

3 onions, divided

2 sprigs fresh thyme

3/4 cup (175 ml) butter, divided

1/2 cup (125 ml) heavy or whipping 35% cream

4 tbsp (60 ml) sliced almonds

1/2 bunch fresh tarragon, coarsely chopped + extra for garnish

Not only is this sauce delicious, it shares its name with my girlfriend…

SERVINGS	PREP TIME	COOKING TIME
2	20 minutes	15 minutes

Preheat oven to 425°F (220°C).

Place halibut pieces on aluminum foil, add salt and drizzle with olive oil.

Slice 1/2 onion. Cover halibut with onion slices and sprigs of thyme, then seal foil to form a pouch. Set aside.

Coarsely chop the remaining 2 1/2 onions into chunks. In a medium saucepan, melt 2 tbsp (30 ml) butter over medium heat. Add chopped onion and 1/4 cup (60 ml) water. Add salt and pepper and stir. Cook, covered, for 3 minutes or until onions are soft and liquid has completely evaporated.

Transfer onions to a blender or food processor and purée until smooth. Pour in cream and blend.

Bake halibut in the oven for 12 minutes.

Meanwhile, heat the rest of the butter in a small skillet. Add the almonds and toast them, until well toasted (browned). Add tarragon and remove from heat.

Take fish out of the oven. Remove the skin (if it doesn't come off easily, the halibut is not fully cooked).

Serve fish with onion purée and browned butter. Garnish with chopped tarragon leaves.

BARBECUED SEA BREAM WITH GREEK SALAD

GRILLED SEA BREAM

3 whole sea breams, cleaned and scaled

Fleur de sel

3 lemons, sliced

1 bunch fresh dill

1 bunch fresh parsley

3 sprigs fresh rosemary

Extra virgin olive oil, for drizzling

2 tbsp (30 ml) freshly squeezed lemon juice

GREEK SALAD

3 red tomatoes, cut into 8 wedges

2 cucumbers, cut into irregular shapes

1 green pepper, cut into irregular shapes

1 red onion, finely chopped

15 kalamata olives

1/2 bunch fresh parsley, chopped

1 tbsp (15 ml) Greek seasoning blend

7-oz (210 g) block feta cheese, cubed

2/3 cup (150 ml) red wine vinegar

2/3 cup (150 ml) extra virgin olive oil, or to taste

I had the chance to prepare this feast on a beautiful beach in Greece for the founder of La Belle Excuse olive oil company. Lots of Greek wine and lasting memories…

SERVINGS	PREP TIME	COOKING TIME
4 to 6	30 minutes	15 to 20 minutes

For the sea bream: Preheat barbecue to medium-high.

With a knife, make 5 or 6 cuts into fish without cutting too deeply. Season interior and exterior of fish with fleur de sel. Stuff fish with lemon slices and herbs, then drizzle generously with oil.

Place fish on the grill and cook for 6 to 8 minutes on each side, until skin is golden brown. Transfer to a serving platter and sprinkle with lemon juice and olive oil.

For the Greek salad: Meanwhile, combine all ingredients in a large salad bowl. Serve with the sea breams.

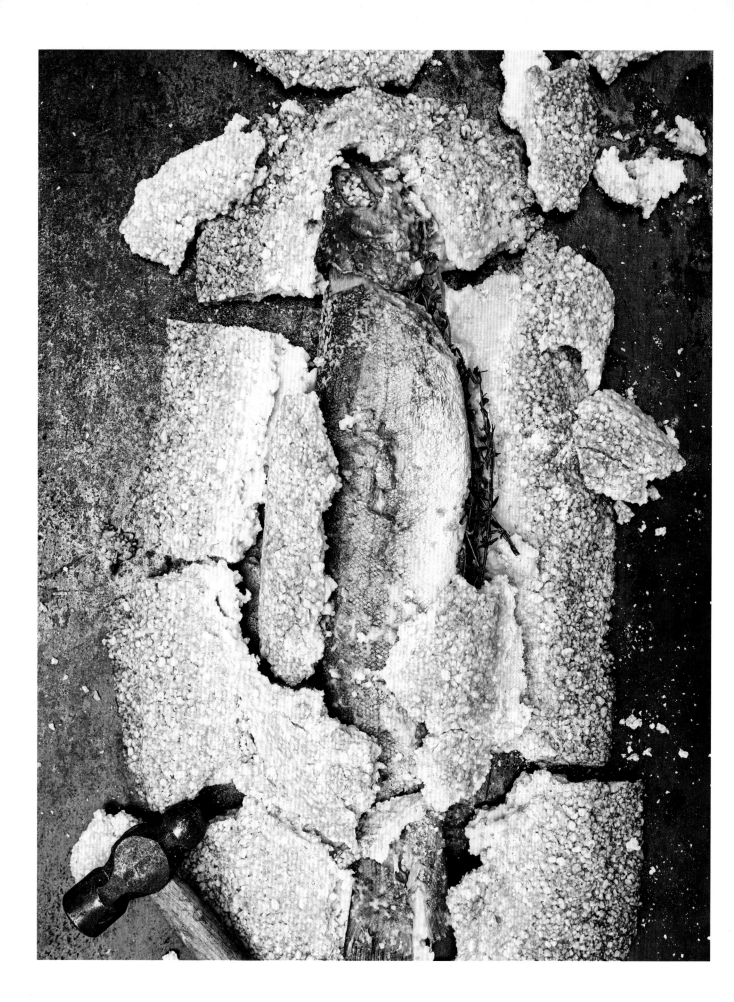

RAINBOW TROUT IN A SALT CRUST

INGREDIENTS

5 lbs (2.5 kg) coarse sea salt (about 8 cups/2 L)

1/2 cup (125 ml) all-purpose flour

6 large egg whites

1 whole rainbow trout with scales (about 2 lbs 10 oz/1.3 kg)

Salt and freshly ground black pepper

3 sprigs fresh thyme

3 sprigs fresh rosemary

3 bay leaves

4 to 5 lemon slices

Freshly squeezed lemon juice, for drizzling

2 tbsp (30 ml) extra virgin olive oil

Toast or crostini, to serve

I'm very happy with the video of this recipe, but it was definitely the first and last time I cooked outdoors in temperatures as low as -22°F (-30°C). Luckily, I still have all my fingers!

SERVINGS	PREP TIME	COOKING TIME
4	20 minutes	25 to 30 minutes

Preheat oven to 450°F (230°C).

In a bowl, mix coarse salt and flour. Add egg whites and 1/4 cup (60 ml) water. With your hands or a spoon, mix well.

With scissors, remove fins from trout (or ask the fishmonger to do it).

Sprinkle salt and pepper inside fish. Stuff with thyme, rosemary, bay leaves and lemon.

Put half of the salt-flour mixture on a piece of parchment paper. Place the fish on top and cover it with the remaining mixture. Press the salt-flour mixture firmly around the fish, making sure the crust is sealed.

Place on a baking sheet and bake for 25 to 30 minutes.

With a mallet, break the salt crust and remove fish. Remove skin and bones.

Place trout fillets on a serving platter. Drizzle with lemon juice and oil. Season to taste with salt and pepper. Serve with toast or crostini.

STRIPED BASS WITH CILANTRO SAUCE VIERGE

INGREDIENTS

1 striped bass (about 2 lbs/1 kg)

1 shallot, chopped

1 bay leaf

1/2 lemon, sliced

A few sprigs of fresh thyme

Salt and freshly ground black pepper

Extra virgin olive oil, for drizzling

SAUCE VIERGE

1 cup (250 ml) diced tomatoes

3/4 cup (175 ml) coarsely chopped fresh cilantro

1/4 cup (60 ml) chopped shallot

1/4 cup (60 ml) diced Preserved Lemons (page 26)

2 tbsp (30 ml) coarsely chopped Cerignola olives

2 tbsp (30 ml) capers

1/4 cup (60 ml) extra virgin olive oil

1 tbsp (15 ml) freshly squeezed lemon juice

SERVINGS	PREP TIME	COOKING TIME
4	20 minutes	20 to 25 minutes

Preheat barbecue or oven to 425°F (220°C).

Stuff fish with shallot, bay leaf, lemon and thyme. Season with salt and pepper. Drizzle oil over fish, place it on a large sheet of foil and wrap the foil like a pouch. Barbecue, covered, on the upper grill. (Alternatively, put it in the oven.) Cook for 20 to 25 minutes.

For the sauce vierge: Meanwhile, combine all ingredients in a bowl.

Serve fish with sauce vierge.

MACKEREL ESCABECHE

INGREDIENTS

2 cups + 1 tbsp (515 ml) olive oil, divided

1 onion, coarsely chopped

1 garlic clove, minced

1 sprig fresh thyme

1 bay leaf

2 cups (500 ml) white wine vinegar

11 oz (330 g) mackerel fillets

1 roasted red pepper, peeled and cut in strips

1 cup (250 ml) peas, blanched and hot

1 banana pepper, sliced (optional)

Fresh parsley, chopped (optional)

SERVINGS	PREP TIME	COOKING TIME	MARINATING TIME
4	20 minutes	10 minutes	24 hours

Heat 1 tbsp (15 ml) oil in a saucepan over low heat. Add onion and sauté for 5 minutes. Add garlic, thyme and bay leaf. Sauté for another 3 minutes. Add vinegar and the remaining 2 cups (500 ml) oil. Bring to a boil.

Place fish in a heatproof dish. Pour the boiling mixture over the cold fish. Cool to room temperature, then refrigerate for 24 hours.

Transfer mackerel to a cutting board, then cut it into 2-inch (5 cm) pieces. Place on a serving plate with the red pepper and peas. Garnish with banana pepper and parsley (if using) and serve as an appetizer!

SALMON GRAVLAX AND POTATO CAKE

SALMON GRAVLAX

1/4 cup (60 ml) granulated sugar

2 1/2 tbsp (37 ml) fine table salt

1 lb (500 g) thick Atlantic salmon, with skin on

POTATO CAKE

2 lbs 6 oz (1.2 kg) Russet potatoes (6 large)

1/2 cup (125 ml) clarified butter, melted

Salt

GARNISHES

1 cup (250 ml) sour cream

A few sprigs of fresh dill

A few sprigs of fresh chives

SERVINGS	PREP TIME	COOKING TIME	CURING TIME
4 to 6	40 minutes	1 hour 5 minutes	50 hours

For the salmon gravlax: Combine sugar and salt in a small bowl. Place salmon on a baking sheet and sprinkle with half of the sugar-salt mixture. Refrigerate, uncovered, for 24 hours.

Cover salmon with the remaining sugar-salt mixture and marinate for another 24 hours in the fridge.

Rinse the fish under cold running water and wipe surface. Check for any bones and remove them. Let dry in a cool place for a few hours. Thinly slice.

For the potato cake: Preheat oven to 425°F (220°C).

Peel potatoes and cut into 1/8-inch (3 mm)-thick slices. Brush the bottom of an 8-inch (20 cm) cast-iron skillet with melted butter. Arrange potato slices in layers, creating a rosette. Between each layer, sprinkle with salt and brush with melted butter.

Heat skillet over medium-high heat for 4 to 5 minutes. Place skillet in the oven and bake for 1 hour. Remove from oven and set aside for 15 minutes. Place a large plate on top of the pan, then carefully invert the potato cake onto a plate.

Top with sour cream, gravlax and herbs.

CHAPTER 7

SEAFOOD

RAZOR CLAMS WITH GRANNY SMITH APPLE, GINGER AND SAMPHIRE

RAZOR CLAMS

1 lemon, thinly sliced

4 garlic cloves, thinly sliced

2 to 3 sprigs fresh thyme

1 shallot, thinly sliced

8 razor clams, rinsed under cold running water

3 tbsp (45 ml) olive oil

1/3 cup (75 ml) white wine

SERVINGS	PREP TIME	COOKING TIME
4	20 minutes	5 minutes

Preheat oven to 500°F (260°C).

For the clams: Line a baking sheet with parchment paper or foil and place lemon slices on it. Cover with garlic, thyme and shallot.

Place razor clams on top, evenly spacing them apart. Drizzle oil on top, cover with foil and bake for 3 minutes.

Remove razor clams from the oven and pour wine over top. Return to the oven and bake for another 2 minutes, or until the shells open. Let cool.

Remove the "foot" (the brown tip) and main intestine from each razor clam, keeping only the firm white flesh.

Cut razor clams into fine slices and put into a small mixing bowl. Refrigerate.

Gently split razor clam shells in half, then clean well under cold running water. Keep the four nicest shells for serving.

For the apple vinaigrette: In a medium-sized bowl, mix all ingredients. Season to taste with salt and pepper.

Add 4 to 5 tbsp (60 to 75 ml) of the vinaigrette to the bowl of razor clams and mix.

To serve, place crushed ice on a chilled plate and arrange the four reserved shells in the center. Generously fill each shell with razor clam mixture. Sprinkle with vinaigrette and garnish with chile pepper, chervil and samphire.

APPLE VINAIGRETTE

1 shallot, finely chopped

1 garlic clove, finely chopped

1/2 Granny Smith apple, finely chopped

2 tbsp (30 ml) finely chopped samphire (sea asparagus or sea beans)

1 tbsp (15 ml) finely chopped gingerroot

1 tbsp (15 ml) ground Espelette pepper

3/4 cup (175 ml) extra virgin olive oil

Zest and juice of 1 lemon

Salt and freshly ground black pepper

GARNISHES

1 1/2 cups (375 ml) crushed ice

1 chile pepper, thinly sliced

10 fresh chervil leaves

2 tbsp (30 ml) chopped samphire (sea asparagus or sea beans)

MEDITERRANEAN GRILLED OCTOPUS

INGREDIENTS

2 medium octopuses

1 cup (250 ml) Mediterranean sea salt

5 garlic cloves, crushed

2 hot peppers, cut in half lengthwise

2 lemons, cut in half

1 onion, cut into wedges

1 large tomato, cut into wedges

1 bunch fresh dill

1 bunch fresh parsley

3 tbsp (45 ml) dried oregano

3 tbsp (45 ml) smoked paprika

3 tbsp (45 ml) dried thyme

3 tbsp (45 ml) dried marjoram

1 tbsp (15 ml) black peppercorns

GARNISHES

1 grilled lemon

1/4 cup (60 ml) extra virgin olive oil

My famous controversial TikTok video shows me hitting an octopus against a rock! This technique, designed to tenderize the octopus, is hundreds of years old and still used around the world. In the kitchen, we often use a rolling pin for the same purpose, and the Japanese sometimes hit it with a very firm daikon radish!

SERVINGS	PREP TIME	COOKING TIME
4 to 6	25 minutes	1 hour 10 minutes

In a large bowl, cover octopuses with sea salt and rub vigorously for 3 to 4 minutes.

Rinse octopuses under cold running water to remove all salt. (This process cleans the octopus and removes the "stickiness.") Place octopuses on a cutting board. Using a rolling pin, tenderize the tentacles by pounding each one for 30 seconds.

Bring a large saucepan of salted water to a boil and add all ingredients except octopuses. Reduce heat to medium-low and gently simmer. Plunge octopuses into the water 2 or 3 times before submerging them to prevent legs from sticking to the bottom of the pan or to each other. Cook for 45 to 60 minutes, until tentacles are tender. Set aside in a bowl and let cool. Cut off head and reserve for another use. (You could thinly slice it for an octopus and potato salad.)

Preheat barbecue to medium-high.

Brush octopuses with oil and barbecue for 5 to 6 minutes on each side, until they have nice grill marks. With a knife, separate the legs from the body and transfer to a serving platter. Garnish with lemon and drizzle oil on top.

SHRIMP TACOS

INGREDIENTS

1 tsp (5 ml) ancho chile powder

1 tsp (5 ml) guajillo chile powder

1 tsp (5 ml) onion powder

1 tsp (5 ml) garlic powder

1 tsp (5 ml) chipotle powder

1 tsp (5 ml) ground annatto seeds

1 tsp (5 ml) ground coriander

1 tsp (5 ml) ground cumin

1 tsp (5 ml) ground dried oregano

2 tbsp (30 ml) avocado oil or vegetable oil

2 lbs (1 kg) medium tiger shrimp, shelled and deveined

Juice of 1 lime

TO SERVE

4 to 6 corn tortillas

Tropical Salsa (page 38)

1 radish, thinly sliced, for garnish (optional)

1/2 cup (125 ml) shredded cabbage, for garnish (optional)

3 limes, cut into wedges

You can see the video for this recipe on my TikTok account. It's one of my favorites to this day. Of course, it always tastes better on a beach in Mexico than in a one-bedroom apartment in the big city, but all you have to do is close your eyes and use your imagination…

SERVINGS	PREP TIME	COOKING TIME	MARINATING TIME
4 to 6	25 minutes	5 minutes	20 minutes

In a bowl, combine all ingredients except lime juice. Marinate for 20 minutes.

Heat a large skillet over high heat. Add the mixture and cook shrimp for 2 minutes on each side. Deglaze with lime juice and remove from heat.

Heat corn tortillas. Serve shrimp on tortillas and garnish with tropical salsa, radishes, shredded cabbage (if using) and a lime wedge.

SCALLOP AND CLEMENTINE CRUDO

INGREDIENTS

4 clementines, divided

1 bird's eye chile, finely chopped

1 small shallot, finely chopped

2 tbsp (30 ml) chopped green onions

1 tsp (5 ml) grated or chopped gingerroot

3 tbsp (45 ml) extra virgin olive oil

2 tsp (10 ml) maple syrup or cane sugar

Fleur de sel

Freshly ground black pepper

6 fresh high-quality U-10 scallops

GARNISHES

Zest of 1 clementine

1 tbsp (15 ml) trout eggs

Extra virgin olive oil, for drizzling

The idea for this dish came to me one day while I was strolling around a market in the 11th arrondissement (district) in Paris. A fish and seafood stall was selling fresh scallops in the shell to eat on the spot. I had a few clementines in my bag, and the combination sounded perfect to me. Sitting on a park bench, eating my raw scallops with fleur de sel, a drizzle of olive oil and a little clementine juice… pure happiness. Here is an enhanced version of my park bench recipe.

SERVINGS	PREP TIME
2 to 4	15 minutes

Squeeze the juice of 2 clementines into a small bowl.

Segment the 2 other clementines. To segment a citrus, use a sharp paring knife to trim off the top and bottom. Hold the citrus upright and carefully slice off the peel, following the shape of the fruit. Remove as much of the white pith as possible. Hold the fruit in your palm and carefully make two cuts inside the membrane walls to cut out the segment. Rotate the citrus and repeat until all segments have been removed.

In a bowl, combine clementine segments, chile, shallot, green onions, ginger, oil and maple syrup. Season to taste with fleur de sel and pepper. Refrigerate.

Using a sharp filleting knife, thinly slice scallops and place them on a plate. Season with fleur de sel. Drizzle vinaigrette on top. Finish with clementine zest, trout eggs and a drizzle of oil.

FRIED SCALLOPS WITH SPICY EGGPLANT PURÉE

EGGPLANT PURÉE

2 eggplants

2 tbsp (30 ml) olive oil

1/4 cup (60 ml) sesame seeds, toasted

2 tbsp (30 ml) chopped pickled garlic scapes + pickling juice for drizzling

2 tbsp Marinated Biquinho Pepper marinade (see page 29)

2 tbsp (30 ml) freshly squeezed lemon juice

2 tbsp (30 ml) butter

Salt

FRIED SCALLOPS

2 tbsp (30 ml) olive oil

12 U-15 scallops

1/4 cup (60 ml) butter

1 sprig fresh thyme

Fresh cilantro leaves

Marinated Biquinho Peppers (page 29)

Salt

SERVINGS	PREP TIME	COOKING TIME
2 to 4	30 minutes	30 minutes

Preheat barbecue to high.

For the eggplant purée: Using a fork, prick holes into the eggplants. Brush with oil and place eggplants on the hot barbecue grill. Grill for 25 minutes, until skin is completely charred. Transfer to a plate. Cut eggplants in half lengthwise.

Drizzle oil over flesh, sprinkle with salt and put eggplants back on the barbecue grill. Cook for 2 minutes, or until the flesh is nicely charred. Let cool for 5 minutes.

Remove skin from eggplants (for a slight smoky taste, keep a bit of charred skin on). Transfer the eggplant flesh to a blender and purée until smooth. Add sesame seeds, pickled garlic scapes, biquinho pepper marinade, lemon juice, butter and salt. Blend until smooth. Set aside.

For the scallops: Heat oil in a hot skillet over medium-high heat. Generously salt scallops, then add them to pan and sear for 2 minutes. Add butter and thyme, flip scallops and baste them. Cook for 1 minute.

On a large serving platter, make 7 nests of eggplant purée and arrange scallops on top.

Garnish with marinated biquinho peppers and cilantro, then add a drizzle of garlic scape pickling juice.

SAUCY OYSTERS

SERVINGS	PREP TIME	COOKING TIME
2 or 3	30 minutes	15 minutes

OYSTERS

4 large Pacific or 12 small Atlantic oysters

Coarse sea salt (optional)

MORNAY SAUCE

1 tbsp (15 ml) butter

1/3 cup (75 ml) all-purpose flour

1 cup (250 ml) milk

1/2 cup (125 ml) grated cheese, such as Gruyère or Emmental

1 tsp (5 ml) Dijon mustard

1 large egg yolk

1/4 broccoli, blanched and coarsely chopped

GARNISHES

1/4 cup (60 ml) panko crumbs

Freshly ground black pepper

For the oysters: Steam oysters in a steamer for 3 to 5 minutes, until they open. Remove oyster meat, cut into chunks and refrigerate.

Line a baking sheet with coarse salt or foil so oysters are stable during cooking. Clean oyster shells and arrange them on the sheet.

For the Mornay sauce: In a saucepan, melt butter over low heat. Blend in flour and cook for 2 minutes. Whisk milk in gradually, mixing until smooth. Cook for 4 minutes. Remove from heat and add cheese, mustard and egg yolk.

Add oysters and broccoli to the Mornay sauce. Pour sauce into the shells on the baking sheet.

Preheat oven to broil.

Sprinkle panko crumbs on the oysters and add pepper. Place the pan in the oven and let the oysters brown for a few minutes. Serve immediately.

CALAMARI STUFFED WITH PAELLA RICE

SERVINGS	PREP TIME	COOKING TIME
4 to 6	45 minutes	40 minutes

PIQUILLO PEPPER COULIS

1 x (about 7-oz/200 g) jar roasted piquillo peppers in oil, drained with 2 tbsp (30 ml) oil reserved

1 tbsp (15 ml) sherry vinegar

Salt and freshly ground black pepper

CALAMARI STUFFED WITH PAELLA RICE

8 whole calamari (about 1 lb 2 oz/560 g), cleaned and heads separated

2 tbsp (30 ml) olive oil, divided

3 1/2 oz (100 g) chorizo

1/2 white onion, diced

1/2 red pepper, diced

3 garlic cloves, finely chopped

2 tbsp (30 ml) sweet paprika

1 cup + 2 tbsp (280 ml) Bomba paella rice

1 tomato, diced

Pinch saffron, steeped in 7 tbsp (105 ml) lukewarm water

1 1/2 cups (375 ml) chicken stock

Salt and freshly ground black pepper

For the piquillo pepper coulis: In a blender, combine the peppers, vinegar and 1/2 cup (125 ml) water. Blend until smooth. Add a little more water if the purée is too thick. Season to taste with salt and pepper. Cover and keep at room temperature.

For the calamari: Bring 6 cups (1.5 L) lightly salted water in a medium saucepan. Dip the calamari bodies in the boiling water for a few seconds, or until they inflate slightly. Transfer to a bowl of ice water to stop the cooking. Store in the fridge.

Heat 1 tbsp (15 ml) oil in a medium saucepan over medium heat. Add chorizo and brown for 4 to 5 minutes, until fat has rendered. Add onion and red pepper and brown for 5 minutes, or until onion is translucent. Add garlic and paprika and stir for 2 minutes. Add rice and sauté for 3 to 4 minutes.

Add tomato, saffron-infused water and stock. Bring to a boil, then reduce heat to low and cook for 6 to 7 minutes. Add calamari heads and cook for another 6 to 8 minutes. Transfer mixture to a baking sheet and let cool to room temperature.

With a pastry bag or a spoon, stuff calamari tubes with rice, leaving enough space to close the opening with a toothpick.

Heat the remaining 1 tbsp (15 ml) oil in a large skillet. Add the calamari and sear on all sides for 5 minutes, or until nicely browned. Remove from heat and set aside.

For the garnishes: Melt butter in a small saucepan over medium heat. Add peas and sauté until heated through. On a large plate, spread out a generous amount of piquillo pepper coulis. Place stuffed calamari on top, then peas on top of the calamari. Finish with lemon juice and lemon zest, parsley (if using) and a drizzle of olive oil.

GARNISHES

1 knob of butter

1/4 cup (60 ml) fresh or frozen peas, blanched in salted water

Zest and juice of 1 lemon

1/2 bunch fresh parsley, chopped (optional)

1 tbsp (15 ml) extra virgin olive oil

Hôtel St-Cerny, Verchères,
Quebec, Canada, 1959.

Wedding celebration at the
Hôtel St-Cerny, Verchères,
Quebec, Canada, 1954.

*Granny Alice (right) holding a shrimp-studded cabbage,
and Mrs. Racine holding crudités.*

Grandpa Lucien and Granny Alice at Au Lutin, a Montreal restaurant
in the 1950s. Granny Alice is bottle-feeding a suckling pig,
which was the tradition at this restaurant.

CHAPTER 8

MEAT

CREAMED CHICKEN

INGREDIENTS

1/2 cup (125 ml) butter

1 x (3 1/2-lbs/1.5 kg) chicken

Salt and freshly ground black pepper

1 lb (500 g) button mushrooms, cut in quarters

8 oz (250 g) wild mushrooms (chanterelles and oyster)

6 shallots, minced (about 8 oz/250 g)

1 head of garlic, cut in half

1 bunch fresh thyme

1 cup (250 ml) white wine, divided

3 cups (750 ml) heavy or whipping 35% cream

Handful of fresh parsley, chopped (optional)

SERVINGS	PREP TIME	COOKING TIME
4 to 6	20 minutes	1 hour 15 minutes

Preheat oven to 425°F (220°C).

Melt butter in a large skillet over medium-high heat. Season the chicken generously with salt and pepper. Add chicken to skillet and brown on all sides for 5 minutes.

Transfer chicken to a casserole dish.

In the same skillet, add mushrooms, shallots, garlic and thyme and cook for 3 to 5 minutes, until mushrooms are browned. Deglaze with 3/4 cup (175 ml) wine, then simmer for 5 to 6 minutes, until reduced by half. Stir in cream. Pour mixture over chicken and bake for 30 minutes.

Reduce the oven temperature to 350°F (180°C) and bake for another 30 minutes.

Remove chicken from the casserole dish and set aside to rest on a plate. Meanwhile, reduce sauce for a few minutes over medium heat. Remove from heat, then add the remaining 1/4 cup (60 ml) wine (for extra flavor).

Cut chicken into pieces, then transfer to a serving platter. Serve with sauce and garnish with parsley (if using).

STEAK TARTARE WITH WHELKS

INGREDIENTS

11 oz (330 g) high-quality beef shoulder or inside round steak

1/2 shallot, chopped

1 tsp (5 ml) salt

1 tbsp (15 ml) capers, rinsed and chopped

1 tbsp (15 ml) chopped samphire (sea asparagus or sea beans)

1 tbsp (15 ml) extra virgin olive oil

Handful of fresh parsley, chopped

Hot sauce to taste

Freshly ground black pepper to taste

GARNISHES

4 oz (125 g) whelks in brine, minced

Zest and juice of 1/2 lemon

4 quail eggs (see Note)

Samphire (sea asparagus or sea beans)

I created this recipe for a pop-up at the Bar St-Denis restaurant. It's my cold version of surf and turf, and you'll be amazed at how good it is!

SERVINGS	PREP TIME
4 (appetizer)	30 minutes

Finely grind the beef or ask the butcher to do it.

In a bowl, combine beef and the remaining ingredients. Spread the beef on a serving plate.

For the garnishes: In a small bowl, mix whelks, lemon zest and lemon juice. Sprinkle whelk mixture over the beef.

Separate quail egg yolks from whites. Put yolks back into the shell and use them to decorate the plate. (Reserve the whites for another use.) Garnish with samphire and add egg yolks to the tartare just before eating!

Note: The elderly, people who are pregnant or living with a compromised immune system, and young children should avoid raw eggs.

TACOS AL PASTOR

TACOS

2 lbs (1 kg) pork shoulder
(butt roast)

Corn tortillas

Grilled Pineapple Salsa Verde
(page 37)

Radishes, thinly sliced

Pineapple, diced (optional)

Red onion, diced

A few fresh cilantro sprigs

Lime wedges

PORK MARINADE

4 or 5 garlic cloves

1 habanero pepper, seeded and
coarsely chopped

1 onion, coarsely chopped

1 dried chile de arbol

1/4 pineapple, peeled, cored and
coarsely chopped

1 cup (250 ml) packed fresh
cilantro sprigs

1/4 cup (60 ml) al pastor
seasoning mix

Juice of 4 or 5 limes

Salt

I don't know if I believe in love at first sight, but the first time I saw this famous sculpture of marinated pork slices turning on a spit, with pineapple for a hat, I knew immediately that we were made for each other. This less traditional version of the dish, adapted for home cooking, will make you the hero of your next Mexican fiesta.

SERVINGS	PREP TIME	COOKING TIME	FREEZING TIME
8 to 10	45 minutes	10 minutes	20 minutes

MARINATING TIME
minimum 1 hour, maximum 24 hours

For the tacos: Place pork in the freezer for 20 minutes. Using a sharp knife, cut pork into 1/2-inch (1 cm)-thick slices. Set aside in a bowl.

For the pork marinade: In a blender or food processor, mix all ingredients until smooth. Pour over pork slices and marinate in the fridge for at least 1 hour and up to 24 hours.

Preheat barbecue to high.

Place pork on the grill and grill for 3 minutes on each side, or until you see some nice grill marks. Transfer pork to a cutting board and finely slice, al pastor–style.

Serve in warm tortillas. Garnish with salsa verde, radishes, pineapple (if using), red onion and cilantro. Serve with lime wedges.

MAPLE PORK SHANK
WITH BUTTERED CABBAGE

MAPLE PORK SHANK

1 x (1 to 1 1/2-lbs/500 to 750 g) pork shank

2 tbsp (30 ml) olive oil

1 white onion, finely chopped

1 large carrot, thinly sliced

3 to 4 garlic cloves, finely chopped

2 to 3 sprigs fresh thyme

2 fresh bay leaves

1/4 cup (60 ml) maple whiskey or regular whiskey

1 cup (250 ml) white wine

4 cups (1 L) pork stock

1/2 cup (125 ml) maple syrup

Salt and freshly ground black pepper

SERVINGS	PREP TIME	COOKING TIME	RESTING TIME
4	25 minutes	4 hours 30 minutes	10 minutes

For the pork shank: Preheat oven to 350°F (180°C).

Using a sharp knife, make notches in pork shank on all sides.

Heat oil in an ovenproof skillet over medium-high heat. Add shank and sear on all sides for 8 to 10 minutes, until browned and crispy. Add onion, carrot, garlic, thyme and bay leaves and cook for 5 minutes, until vegetables are softened.

Deglaze with whiskey and flambé until flames burn out. Add wine and simmer for 3 to 4 minutes, until reduced by half. Add stock and maple syrup and bring to a boil. Put the skillet in the oven and bake for at least 3 1/2 hours, turning the shank every 30 to 40 minutes.

For the buttered cabbage: Meanwhile, bring a saucepan of salted water to a boil, add the cabbage and blanch for 2 to 3 minutes. Transfer to a strainer, drain and let cool.

Heat a large skillet over medium-high heat. Cook lardons for 8 to 10 minutes, until browned and crispy. Transfer to a strainer (reserving the fat for another use).

Add oil and half the butter to the same skillet over medium heat. Add onion, carrot, garlic, bay leaves, salt and pepper and sauté for 10 minutes, or until vegetables are tender. Add cabbage and cook for 2 minutes. Return lardons to skillet. Add wine and simmer for 5 minutes, until reduced by three-quarters. Add stock and bring to a boil.

Cover and cook for 25 to 30 minutes, until cabbage is tender. Stir in the remaining butter, cover and set aside to rest for 10 minutes.

Remove pork shank from the oven. Serve it on a nest of the buttered cabbage. Drizzle with pan juices.

BUTTERED CABBAGE

1 green cabbage, thinly sliced

5 oz (150 g) pork lardons

1 tbsp (15 ml) olive oil

1/2 cup (125 ml) butter, divided

1 white onion, finely chopped

1 large carrot, thinly sliced

3 or 4 garlic cloves, thinly sliced

2 fresh bay leaves

1 cup (250 ml) white wine

1 1/4 cups (310 ml) vegetable stock

Salt and freshly ground black pepper

TURKEY LEG WITH MAPLE REDUCTION

SERVINGS	PREP TIME	COOKING TIME	RESTING TIME
2	20 minutes	2 hours 30 minutes	25 minutes

TURKEY

1 large turkey leg

3 tbsp (45 ml) olive oil, divided

Salt and freshly ground black pepper

11 tbsp (165 ml) butter, divided

4 to 5 garlic cloves, peeled and crushed

1 shallot, cut in half lengthwise

1 bunch fresh rosemary

1 bunch fresh thyme

3/4 cup (175 ml) cranberries, thawed if frozen

1 cup (250 ml) white wine

1 1/4 cups (310 ml) turkey or chicken stock

REDUCTION

1 cup (250 ml) maple syrup

1 sprig fresh rosemary

2 tbsp (30 ml) Dijon mustard

GARNISH

1/2 bunch fresh chives, chopped

For the turkey: Preheat oven to 400°F (200°C).

Baste turkey with 2 tbsp (30 ml) oil and generously season with salt. Heat the remaining 1 tbsp (15 ml) oil in a large ovenproof skillet over medium-high heat. Add turkey, skin side down, and sear for 5 to 6 minutes, until skin is nicely browned. Turn over leg and cook for another 5 to 6 minutes, until browned.

Remove oil from the skillet. Add 7 tbsp (105 ml) butter, garlic, shallot, rosemary and thyme. With a spoon, continuously baste turkey with butter for 2 to 3 minutes. Add cranberries, deglaze with wine and cook for 3 to 4 minutes, until reduced by half. Add stock, then simmer for 20 minutes.

For the reduction: Meanwhile, add maple syrup and rosemary to a small saucepan and reduce over medium heat by half. Stir in mustard. Let cool completely. With a brush, generously baste turkey leg with the maple syrup reduction.

Reduce the oven temperature to 350°F (180°C). Roast turkey for 1 1/2 hours, or until it reaches an internal temperature of 165°F (75°C). Baste turkey with leftover maple syrup reduction every 15 to 20 minutes. Add water or stock if the pan gets too dry. Transfer turkey to a wire rack and rest for at least 25 minutes. Reserve cooked shallots for garnish.

Place a sieve over a small saucepan. Strain the contents of the skillet through the sieve to collect the cooking juices. Bring to a boil and reduce until the sauce is thick enough to coat the back of a spoon. Remove from heat and add the remaining 4 tbsp (60 ml) butter. Whisk the sauce, using a circular motion to emulsify.

Serve on a root vegetable purée, pour a generous amount of sauce on top and garnish with cooked shallots and fresh chives.

DUCK BREAST WITH BEETS

SERVINGS	PREP TIME	COOKING TIME
2	40 minutes	45 minutes

INGREDIENTS

4 red beets

2 sprigs fresh thyme, divided

2 sprigs fresh rosemary, divided

6 garlic cloves, peeled and crushed, divided

Fleur de sel

1/2 cup (125 ml) champagne or other sparkling wine

2 tbsp heavy or whipping 35% cream

2 tbsp (30 ml) olive oil, divided

1 duck breast

1 tbsp (15 ml) butter

1/4 cup (60 ml) balsamic glaze

1 tbsp (15 ml) chopped chives (optional)

In a saucepan, combine beets, a sprig each of thyme and rosemary, 3 garlic cloves and a pinch of fleur de sel. Add enough water to cover and cook over medium-high heat for 20 to 25 minutes, until a knife can be easily inserted into a beet.

Drain beets, then cool for 5 minutes. Carefully peel them while they are still hot. Dice 1 beet and set aside for garnish.

In a food processor, combine the remaining beets, champagne, cream, 1 tbsp (15 ml) oil and a little fleur de sel and process until smooth. Set aside.

Preheat oven to 400°F (200°C).

With a sharp knife, remove tendons and excess fat from duck breast. Make notches in the fat without cutting into the breast. Sprinkle with salt.

Place duck breast, skin side down, in a cold nonstick ovenproof skillet. Heat the skillet over medium-high heat and sear duck until crispy and a lot of fat has been rendered. Pour excess fat 2 or 3 times into a bowl and reserve for another use (such as duck-roasted potatoes). Flip the duck.

Add butter, the remaining sprigs of rosemary and thyme and 3 garlic cloves. Using a brush, baste duck skin with balsamic glaze. Roast in the oven for 4 to 5 minutes, until the desired doneness. Set aside the duck to rest on a baking sheet for 6 minutes. Cut the duck breast into 4 or 5 slices lengthwise.

Heat the remaining 1 tbsp (15 ml) oil in a small skillet. Add reserved beets and sauté for 3 minutes.

In a shallow dish, make a nest of beet purée and fan duck slices on top. Garnish with beets, a pinch of fleur de sel and chives (if using).

RABBIT WITH MUSTARD SAUCE

INGREDIENTS

3 oz (90 g) morels

2 large rabbits

Salt and freshly ground black pepper

Olive oil, for drizzling

2 tbsp (30 ml) butter

8 oz (250 g) chanterelles, cut into quarters, or whole if small

3 garlic cloves, finely chopped

1 shallot, chopped

1 cup (250 ml) white wine

2 cups (500 ml) heavy or whipping 35% cream

2 tbsp (30 ml) Dijon mustard, divided

2 tbsp (30 ml) mustard seeds, divided

2 tbsp (30 ml) maple syrup

10 to 12 fresh parsley leaves, chopped

1 bunch fresh chives, chopped

To this day, whenever someone asks me what my favorite dish of all time is, this is the one I choose. I don't know if it was the meal itself, the people I was with, the service or simply the fact that I was sitting on a fantastic patio next to the famous Avignon Bridge in the south of France, but rabbit is f*** delicious and you have to try it! Here, it is prepared with a creamy mustard sauce and garnished with a good amount of wild mushrooms.

SERVINGS	PREP TIME	COOKING TIME
4 to 6	20 minutes	50 minutes

Preheat oven to 350°F (180°C).

Rinse morels. Plunge them in boiling water for 30 seconds, then place on a clean tea towel to dry. Set aside.

Sprinkle rabbits with salt and pepper, then drizzle with oil.

Heat a roasting pan over medium-high heat. Add rabbits and sear for 6 to 8 minutes, until all sides are browned. Set aside on a baking sheet.

Melt butter in the same pan over high heat. Add both mushrooms and sauté for 5 minutes. Season with salt and pepper. Add garlic and shallot and cook for 2 minutes. Deglaze with wine and cook for 3 to 4 minutes, until liquid has reduced by half. Stir in cream, 1 tbsp (15 ml) Dijon mustard and 1 tbsp (15 ml) mustard seeds and bring to a boil.

In a bowl, mix the remaining 1 tbsp (15 ml) mustard, 1 tbsp (15 ml) mustard seeds and maple syrup. Baste this mixture over all sides of the rabbits.

Return the rabbits to the roasting pan and bake for 40 minutes. Baste with sauce every 10 minutes.

Place rabbits on a large serving platter and drizzle creamy mustard sauce on top. Garnish with parsley and chives and enjoy!

BARBECUED LAMB STEAKS

MARINADE

1 lemon, cut in half

3 garlic cloves, minced

1 small onion, minced

2 tbsp (30 ml) olive oil

2 tbsp (30 ml) Aleppo pepper

2 tbsp (30 ml) smoked paprika

1 tbsp (15 ml) salt

Freshly ground black pepper

LAMB STEAKS

2 x (12-oz/375 g) lamb leg steaks

Aleppo pepper flakes

Tomato salad, to serve

SERVINGS	PREP TIME	COOKING TIME	MARINATING TIME
2	15 minutes	10 minutes	12 hours

For the marinade: Gently squeeze most of the juice from lemon into a large bowl. Set lemon aside. Add the remaining marinade ingredients to the bowl and mix.

For the lamb steaks: Place lamb steaks in the bowl and coat well with marinade. Cover and marinate in the fridge for 12 hours.

Preheat barbecue to high.

Place lamb steaks on the grill directly over the fire and sear both sides to mark them. Transfer steaks to the upper grill and cook for another 5 to 7 minutes. Add lemon, cut sides down, and grill while the lamb finishes cooking.

Transfer lamb steaks to a serving plate. Squeeze grilled lemon over steaks and garnish with Aleppo pepper flakes.

Serve with a tomato salad.

BREADED PORK CUTLETS

PARSLEY BREAD CRUMBS

1/2 cup (125 ml) bread crumbs

1 cup (250 ml) lightly packed fresh parsley, coarsely chopped

PORK CUTLETS

12 oz (375 g) pork loin, cut into 4 slices, about 1/4 inch (0.5 cm) thick

Salt and freshly ground black pepper

1/2 cup (125 ml) all-purpose flour

1 large egg

5 tsp (25 ml) whole milk

1 tbsp (15 ml) Dijon mustard

3 tbsp (45 ml) butter

1 tbsp (15 ml) olive oil

1 lemon, cut in half

1 large pickle, thinly sliced lengthwise

SERVINGS	PREP TIME	COOKING TIME
2	30 minutes	10 minutes

For the parsley bread crumbs: In a food processor, mix bread crumbs and parsley until mixture is green. Set aside on a plate.

For the pork cutlets: With a meat tenderizer, flatten cutlets by half. Season with salt and pepper on both sides.

Spread flour on a plate. In a shallow bowl, beat together egg, milk and mustard. Dip a cutlet into the flour, then shake to remove the excess. Dip it fully in the egg mixture, then dip it in bread crumbs. Repeat with the remaining cutlets.

Heat butter and oil in a large skillet over medium heat, until butter foams. Gently place cutlets in the skillet and cook for 2 to 3 minutes. Turn, then cook for another 2 to 3 minutes, until nicely browned.

Serve with lemon wedges and pickle slices.

PRIME RIB AND GARLIC ESCARGOTS

INGREDIENTS

1 x (2 lb/1 kg) prime rib, 2 inches (5 cm) thick

10 shallots, cut in quarters

1 x (750 ml) bottle red wine

1 tbsp (15 ml) red wine vinegar

1/2 cup (125 ml) butter, softened

1/4 bunch fresh parsley, chopped

3 garlic cloves, finely chopped

Salt and freshly ground black pepper

1 x (4 oz/125 g) can escargots, rinsed and drained (see Note)

Pan-fried thyme, to garnish (optional)

Wandering the streets of Amsterdam one warm fall day, looking for a natural wine bar, my girlfriend and I stumbled upon GlouGlou. With a glass of Burgundy in hand, we ordered garlic escargots and prime rib. The intermingled flavors of these two dishes gave me the idea of combining them on the same plate.

SERVINGS	PREP TIME	COOKING TIME	RESTING TIME
4 to 6	10 minutes	30 minutes	2 hours and 15 minutes

Let the prime rib rest at room temperature for 2 hours before cooking.

In a saucepan, combine shallots, wine and vinegar and bring to a boil over medium-high heat. Reduce heat to low and cook until wine has almost completely evaporated.

In a bowl, mix butter, parsley, garlic, salt and pepper. Set aside 1/4 cup (60 ml) of this mixture for the escargots and roll up the rest in plastic wrap. Refrigerate.

Wrap escargots and the 1/4 cup (60 ml) of the garlic-butter mixture in aluminum foil. Set aside.

Preheat barbecue to high.

Generously salt both sides of the prime rib, then sear both sides on the barbecue until it has grill marks. Grill on low heat on the upper grill for 8 minutes per side.

Put foil-wrapped escargots on the upper grill grate and cook for 9 minutes, until both sides are seared and cooked through. Meanwhile, take beef off the barbecue and let it rest, covered with foil, for 12 minutes. Transfer escargots to a plate.

Cut chilled garlic butter into disks. Slice prime rib and garnish with butter disks, thyme (if using) and escargots.

Note: You can purchase escargots at specialty supermarkets or from reputable online shops such as Peconic Escargot.

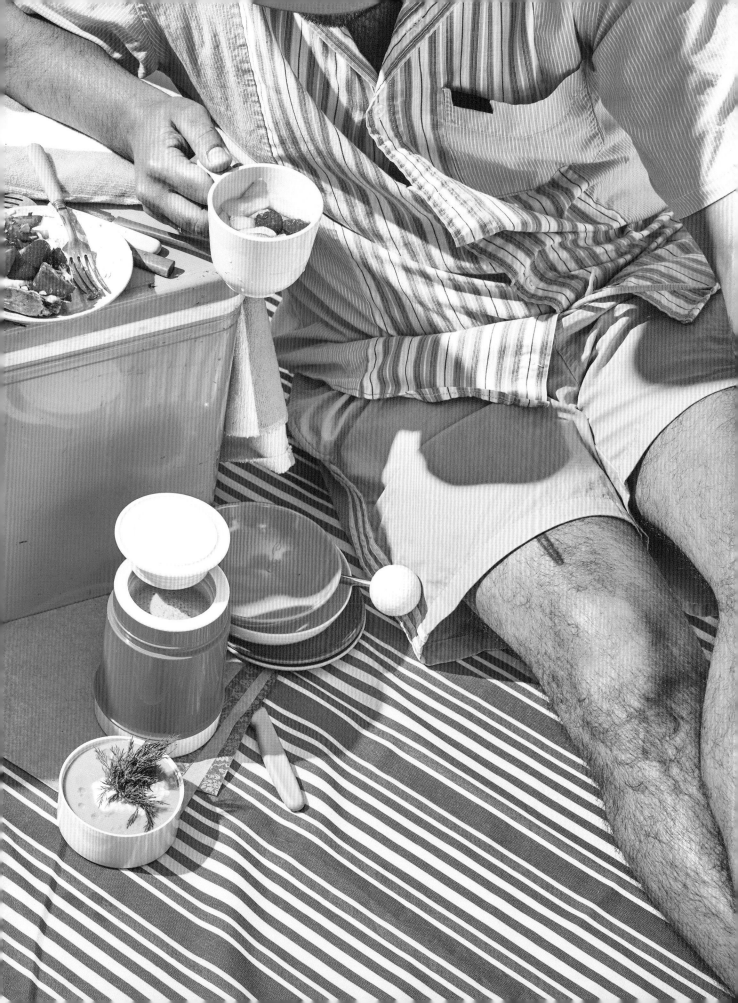

CHAPTER 9

DESSERTS

STRAWBERRY PISTACHIO PIE

PASTRY

2 tbsp (30 ml) ground pistachios

1 3/4 cups (425 ml) all-purpose flour + extra for dusting

1 cup (250 ml) confectioners' (icing) sugar

2/3 cup (150 ml) butter, cubed

1 large egg

Baking beans or pie weights

PISTACHIO FILLING

1 1/4 cups (310 ml) ground pistachios

1 cup + 3 tbsp (295 ml) confectioners' (icing) sugar

1/2 cup (125 ml) butter

3 tbsp (45 ml) all-purpose flour

2 large eggs

GARNISHES

14 oz (400 g) strawberries, cut in quarters

2 tbsp (30 ml) granulated sugar

Whipped cream

Chopped pistachios

I have a small confession to make: I have a massive sweet tooth and I am not proud to admit that I have eaten this entire pie in a single evening. Delicious but dangerous.

SERVINGS	PREP TIME	COOKING TIME	REFRIGERATION TIME
6 to 8	40 minutes	30 minutes	1 hour 30 minutes

For the pastry: In a food processor, mix pistachios, flour and sugar. Add butter and pulse until the mixture has a sandy texture. Add egg and pulse a few times, until dough holds together. Wrap in plastic wrap and chill in the fridge for at least 1 hour.

For the pistachio filling: In a food processor, mix all ingredients. Set aside.

Preheat oven to 375°F (190°C).

On a lightly floured work surface, roll out dough with a rolling pin, about 1/8 inch (3 mm) thick. Line a 10-inch (25 cm) pie plate with the dough. Using a knife, trim along edges. Refrigerate for 30 minutes.

Place a piece of parchment paper over dough and put baking beans or pie weights on top to prevent dough from puffing up during baking. Blind-bake for 15 minutes. Remove paper and weights. Reduce the oven temperature to 350°F (180°C). Spread the pistachio filling in the pie crust and bake for 12 minutes. Cool at room temperature.

For the garnishes: Combine strawberries and sugar and set aside for 3 minutes to macerate. Top with whipped cream, then add strawberries. Garnish with chopped pistachios.

BLONDIES WITH BLUEBERRY SAUCE

SERVINGS	PREP TIME	COOKING TIME
4 to 6	15 minutes	30 minutes

BLONDIES

1/2 cup (125 ml) butter + extra for greasing the pan

1/3 cup + 2 tbsp (105 ml) white chocolate chips, divided

2 large eggs

1 cup (250 ml) packed brown sugar

1 cup (250 ml) sifted all-purpose flour

Whipping 35% cream or ice cream, to serve

BLUEBERRY SAUCE

1/2 cup (125 ml) granulated sugar

1 cup (250 ml) blueberries

1/4 cup (60 ml) cold butter

Lemon zest

For the blondies: Preheat oven to 350°F (180°C). Grease an 8-inch (20 cm) square cake pan.

In the microwave or a double boiler, melt butter and 1/3 cup (75 ml) white chocolate chips. Set aside.

In a food processor, combine eggs and brown sugar and blend on high speed for 4 minutes. Add flour and mix gently.

Using a spatula, fold the melted chocolate mixture into the egg–brown sugar mixture.

Pour the mixture into the prepared pan and sprinkle the remaining 2 tbsp (30 ml) chocolate chips on top. Bake for 20 minutes. Remove from oven and let cool.

For the blueberry sauce: In a skillet, combine sugar and 1/2 cup (125 ml) water and bring to a boil over medium-high heat. Add blueberries and cook for 3 minutes.

Gently crush blueberries with the back of a spoon. Cook for another 1 to 2 minutes, then remove from heat. Using a whisk, blend butter into the sauce.

Unmold the blondie onto a plate. Spoon blueberry sauce on top and garnish with lemon zest. Serve with whipping cream or ice cream.

FRENCH CUSTARD TART

PASTRY DOUGH

1/2 cup (125 ml) butter

1 cup + 2 tbsp (280 ml) all-purpose flour + extra for dusting

Pinch salt

Baking beans or pie weights

CUSTARD

3/4 cup (175 ml) whole milk

3/4 cup + 2 tbsp (205 ml) sweetened condensed milk

5 large egg yolks

GARNISHES

Whipped cream

Dulce de leche

Maple flakes or sprinkles (optional)

This dessert, from the menu for my pop-up event at Bar St-Denis in Montreal, was just too good not to include in my book.

SERVINGS	PREP TIME	COOKING TIME	RESTING TIME
4 to 6	40 minutes	1 hour 45 minutes	2 hours

For the pastry dough: In a bowl, combine butter, flour and salt. Make a well in center and pour in 1/4 cup (60 ml) cold water. Mix with your hands until a ball of dough forms. Wrap in plastic wrap and let rest for at least 1 hour.

On a lightly floured work surface, roll out the dough with a rolling pin, about 1/4 inch (0.5 cm) thick. Line an 8-inch (20 cm) pie plate with the dough. Let the dough rest in the fridge for 1 hour.

Preheat oven to 425°F (220°C).

Place a sheet of parchment paper over dough and add baking beans or pie weights on top to prevent dough from puffing up during baking. Blind-bake for 30 minutes, then reduce the oven temperature to 350°F (180°C). Remove the paper and pie weights and bake for 30 minutes. Remove from oven and set aside.

For the custard: Prepare this 15 minutes before the pie shell is completely baked. In a saucepan, combine milk and condensed milk and heat over medium heat, stirring continuously so it doesn't stick to the bottom.

Put egg yolks in a bowl. As soon as milk starts to boil, pour it over the egg yolks while whisking. Strain, then pour into the pie shell.

Reduce the oven temperature to 325°F (160°C) and bake for 40 to 45 minutes, until custard is set. Let cool.

To serve, garnish with whipped cream, dulce de leche and maple flakes (if using).

LEMON CHIFFON CAKE

CHIFFON CAKE

1 cup (250 ml) all-purpose flour

1/4 tsp (1 ml) baking soda

1 cup + 3/4 tsp (253 ml) granulated sugar, divided

1/4 tsp (1 ml) salt

3 large eggs, separated

1/4 cup (60 ml) canola oil

Zest and juice of 1 lemon

1/4 tsp (1 ml) cream of tartar

SERVINGS	PREP TIME	COOKING TIME	REFRIGERATION TIME
6 to 8	4 hours	1 hour	4 to 5 hours

Preheat oven to 350°F (180°C), with rack positioned in middle. Grease an 8-inch (20 cm) square baking pan.

For the chiffon cake: In a bowl, combine flour, baking soda, 1 cup (250 ml) sugar and salt.

In another bowl, combine egg yolks, oil, lemon zest, lemon juice and 1/3 cup (75 ml) water. Using a wooden spoon, mix wet ingredients into dry ingredients.

Using a hand blender, whip egg whites, the remaining 3/4 tsp (3 ml) sugar and cream of tartar until stiff peaks form. Fold gently into the batter. Pour into the prepared pan, then bake for 50 to 60 minutes, until a tester inserted in the center comes out. Let cool completely on a wire rack.

For the lemon custard: In a saucepan, mix all ingredients except butter over low heat for 4 to 5 minutes. Increase the heat to medium and whisk vigorously until mixture is thick enough to coat the back of a spoon.

Remove from heat and whisk in butter, one cube at a time. Pour into a bowl, then cover with plastic wrap. Refrigerate for 2 to 3 hours, until cool.

For the meringue: In a heavy-bottomed saucepan, combine sugar and 1/2 cup (125 ml) water over medium heat and heat to 250°F (120°C).

Using a hand mixer, beating egg whites in a bowl on low speed.

Remove syrup from heat when it reaches 255°F (125°C). Increase the speed on the hand mixer and pour syrup in a thin stream over egg whites. Mix until stiff peaks form. Pour into a pastry bag and place in the fridge.

Pour lemon custard over the cooled cake and spread evenly. Cover with the meringue… be creative! Using a kitchen torch or in the oven broiler, brown the meringue. Refrigerate for at least 2 hours before serving.

LEMON CUSTARD

3 large eggs

4 large egg yolks

1/2 cup (125 ml) granulated sugar

1/4 tsp (1 ml) salt

3/4 cup (175 ml) freshly squeezed
lemon juice

3 tbsp (45 ml) whole milk

1/2 cup (125 ml) cold butter, cut
in large cubes

MERINGUE

1 cup (250 ml) granulated sugar

3 large egg whites, at room
temperature

CHOCOLATE RASPBERRY MOUSSE

INGREDIENTS

6 oz (175 ml) bittersweet (dark) chocolate

1/3 cup (75 ml) hot milk

2 oz (60 ml) Chambord raspberry liqueur

1 large egg yolk

1/2 cup (125 ml) egg whites

2 1/4 tsp (11 ml) granulated sugar

Raspberries

SERVINGS	PREP TIME	COOKING TIME	REFRIGERATION TIME
4	20 minutes	10 minutes	3 hours

Melt chocolate in a double boiler. (Alternatively, melt in a large heatproof bowl placed over a saucepan of gently boiling water, making sure the bowl doesn't touch the water.)

Pour in hot milk and Chambord. In a small bowl, whisk egg yolk. Add 2 tbsp (30 ml) of the hot milk mixture to the egg yolk and whisk. Whisk egg yolk into the hot milk mixture. Remove the pan from the heat.

In a bowl, beat egg whites with sugar until soft peaks form. Add a third of the beaten whites into the chocolate mixture. Whisk vigorously. Gently fold the remaining egg whites into the mixture.

Divide among four bowls and refrigerate for at least 3 hours. Garnish with fresh raspberries and serve.

WHITE CHOCOLATE AND RHUBARB PANNA COTTA

INGREDIENTS

28 g (1 oz) gelatin sheets

1 1/2 cups (375 ml) heavy or whipping 35% cream

1/2 cup (125 ml) whole milk

1 vanilla bean, split lengthwise

3 1/2 oz (100 g) white chocolate, broken in pieces

RHUBARB TOPPING

3 stalks rhubarb, cut into 1/2-inch (1 cm) cubes

1 cup (250 ml) granulated sugar

Panna cotta is my dessert of choice when I have people over for dinner. You can make it ahead of time, and it will chill in the fridge until you garnish it just before serving! You can also give some to your guests to take home at the end of the evening (as long as they bring back the dishes the next time!).

SERVINGS	PREP TIME	COOKING TIME	REFRIGERATION TIME
4 to 6	20 minutes	5 minutes	2 hours 15 minutes

Soak gelatin sheets in ice water to soften them. Remove from water.

In a saucepan, combine cream, milk and vanilla bean and heat over low heat. Do not allow it to boil.

Place chocolate in a deep mixing bowl. Pour the hot milk mixture over chocolate and stir until melted. Add gelatin to the mixture while it is still hot. Divide mixture among four to six and refrigerate for at least 2 hours until set.

For the topping: Place rhubarb in a heatproof bowl. In a saucepan, combine sugar and 1 cup (250 ml) water and heat over medium heat until sugar has dissolved. Pour hot syrup over rhubarb and refrigerate for 15 minutes, until fully cooled.

Garnish panna cotta with rhubarb and save the leftover syrup to make cocktails!

CHAPTER 10

COCKTAILS

RHUBARB NEGRONI

RHUBARB GIN

5 stalks rhubarb

1 bottle (25-oz/700 ml) London dry gin

RHUBARB NEGRONI

1 oz (30 ml) rhubarb gin (see above)

1 oz (30 ml) Suze

1 oz (30 ml) Lillet

1 large ice cube

Strip of rhubarb (optional)

A twist on one of my favorite classic cocktails: my version of the White Negroni! The bitterness already found in this cocktail marries perfectly with that of the rhubarb.

SERVINGS	PREP TIME	INFUSION TIME
1	5 minutes	1 month

For the rhubarb gin: Wash the rhubarb, dice it and put it in Mason jars. Pour in the gin. Infuse as long as possible, ideally 1 month.

For the rhubarb negroni: Into a mixing glass, pour the rhubarb gin, Suze and Lillet over ice. Mix for 20 seconds with a spoon, then pour through a cocktail strainer into an old-fashioned glass. Add a large ice cube. Garnish glass with a strip of rhubarb (if using).

CRUSHED CUCUMBER WITH RUM

LIME SYRUP

Zest of 4 limes

1 1/4 cups (310 ml) granulated sugar

1 1/4 cups (310 ml) freshly squeezed lime juice

CRUSHED CUCUMBER WITH RUM

1 cucumber + a few small chunks for mixing + a few slices for garnish

3 or 4 lime wedges

3 or 4 basil leaves + extra for garnish

5 or 6 mint leaves + extra for garnish

1 1/2 oz (45 ml) dark rum

1 oz (30 ml) lime syrup (see above)

Ice cubes

Sparkling water

SERVINGS	PREP TIME	COOKING TIME	MACERATION TIME
1	5 minutes	3 minutes	1 hour

For the lime syrup: Combine lime zest and sugar in a bowl and set aside to macerate for 1 hour.

In a saucepan, combine sugar-lime zest mixture and lime juice and bring to a boil. Strain, then refrigerate.

For the cocktail: Put cucumber through a juicer and set aside 1 oz (30 ml) of the juice. (If you don't have a juicer, use 4 or 5 cucumber slices crushed in a mortar.)

In a cocktail shaker, combine lime wedges, a few chunks of cucumber, basil and mint and crush. Add rum, lime syrup, the reserved cucumber juice and ice and shake vigorously.

Strain into a glass containing a few ice cubes and add sparkling water. Garnish with cucumber slices and basil and mint leaves.

AMERICANO SHANDY

SERVINGS
2

PREP TIME
5 minutes

INGREDIENTS

3 oz (90 ml) Campari

3 oz (90 ml) Cynar or red vermouth

Ice cubes

1 x (12 1/2-oz/355 ml) can Italian pilsner

2 orange slices

Divide Campari and Cynar between 2 highball glasses. Fill the glasses with ice. Pour in beer. Garnish each glass with an orange slice. Cheers!

MARGARITA WITH ESPELETTE PEPPER

INGREDIENTS

1 lime, sliced

Fine table salt

Ground Espelette pepper

1 1/2 oz (45 ml) tequila

1/4 oz (7 ml) triple sec

1 1/2 tsp (7 ml) freshly squeezed lime juice

A few drops of hot sauce, if desired

1 1/2 tsp (7 ml) confectioners' (icing) sugar

Ice cubes

If I were on a desert island and I had to choose just one cocktail for the rest of my life, it would definitely be a margarita. Add a rim of my favorite chile pepper and my life is complete.

SERVINGS	PREP TIME
1	5 minutes

Moisten the rim of a glass with a lime wedge. Make a mixture of 1 part salt to 1 part Espelette pepper and spread on a small plate. Dip the top of the glass in the salt mixture.

Pour the tequila, triple sec, lime juice, hot sauce (if using) and sugar into a cocktail shaker. Shake vigorously with ice cubes and pour into a glass. Garnish with lime.

FUN PUNCH

INGREDIENTS

4 limes, cut into wedges, divided

1 x (1-inch/2.5 cm) piece gingerroot, thinly sliced

9 oz (280 ml) green Chartreuse

2 x (12 3/4-oz/375 ml) bottles ginger beer

Ice

2 cups (500 ml) raspberries

SERVINGS
4 to 6

PREP TIME
10 minutes

Using a pestle and mortar, combine 3 limes with ginger and crush. Transfer the mixture to a 6-cup (1.5 L) pitcher or punch bowl.

Add Chartreuse and ginger beer. Fill the pitcher or bowl with ice and add raspberries and the remaining lime wedges. Serve and enjoy!

ALMOST A MEZCAL OLD-FASHIONED

INGREDIENTS

2 1/2 oz (75 ml) mezcal

1/2 oz (15 ml) Aperol

1 tbsp (15 ml) agave syrup

4 or 5 drops grapefruit bitters

Large ice cubes

1 twist grapefruit zest

Created by my good friend and former coworker Erik Systad, this variation on a mezcal old-fashioned will impress your guests every time!

SERVINGS	PREP TIME
1	5 minutes

In a large mixing glass, combine mezcal, Aperol, agave syrup and grapefruit bitters. Using a long cocktail spoon, mix well to blend. Fill the glass with large ice cubes. Mix for another minute.

Place a cocktail strainer over a whiskey glass containing a large regular or round ice cube and pour in the mixture. Twist grapefruit zest, swipe it around the rim of the glass, then use it as a garnish.

INDEX

ACKNOWLEDGMENTS

Family: Mom, Pops, Denis, Sylvie B., my grandparents: Mami and Papi St. Cerny, Mami and Papi Dagenais, my three brothers: Maxime, Louis, Alexandre. My godson Arlo, Jackie, Johanne, Claude, Pierre, Anne-Marie, JF, Manon, Bernard, Sylvie D., Paul, Maxime-Olivier, Béatrice, Tatiana, Valérie, Guillaume, David.

Friends: Daniel Walfish, Vincent Gignac, Françis Lapierre, Brian Finn (manfriend), Marie-Wolf, Billie, Kyle Thomas, LP, Ren Rob, Marie-Mich, David and Benjamin Gauthier, Ahmed, Léa, Victor, Zach, Maz, Amanda, Stéphane, the Caudrelier family, Pascale, Simon, the St. Laurent family, Hugo, Étienne, Catherine, Mike, Franck, Erik, Kirk, Richard, Matt, Kyle, Big Bricc, Léonie, Louis T., Jamie N., Yutaka, Cole, Max and Mat Nantais, Aaron, Ian, Vincent D., Mat, Nat, Lauraine, Jade, Mac, Jeff, Jorge, Oli, Yohan, Shawn, Hugo, Yoshi, Robin, Charles, Matt, Andrew, Max, Marty, Jade, Audrey, Mark the Viking, the Francoeur family, David Lee, Giovanni, the Stavropoulos family, Whoogys, Dime, Mehraton, Vans, Traeger.

Publishing team: Brian Finn, Renaud Robert, William Langlais, Isabel Tardif, Ann Châteauvert, Roxane Vaillant, Julien Rodrigue, Florence Bisch, JP and the rest of the team at Groupe Homme.

Dulcedo Agency: Benjamin Carter, Karim S. Leduc, Karim Rekik, Bianca Ricchetti.

Thanks to my brother Max for always supporting me in my various projects and helping me make them happen.

Thanks to Ceragres Tile Group for letting us use their tiles for the photos.

Thanks to my assistant Vincent, who helped me finish the book on time in spite of the tight timelines.

Thanks to Réal Francoeur and his legendary bread oven. Thanks to Couteaux CLK for providing me with the best blades.

Thanks to David and Emily from Bar St-Denis for their incredible help making this book happen.

One thing is for sure: none of this would have been possible without my girlfriend, Amandine. After a few evenings watching me film myself in my tiny kitchen in Old Longueuil, Quebec, she offered to get behind the camera. I was a bit reluctant, but in the end I agreed. I quickly learned that we had something that could go viral.

I feel like it's impossible not to forget someone, so thank you to everyone who contributed directly or indirectly to the production of this book.

Thanks to everyone who has read all the way to the acknowledgments!

Peace!

RIP Mia Van Den Dool, 1990–2021.
RIP Dillon Ojo, 1995–2018.

Laurent Dagenais was born and raised in Montreal where he quickly carved out a space in the culinary scene. With his creativity and one-of-a-kind approach, he aims to pass on techniques in a fun, spirited way by creating playful, easy-to-make and delicious dishes that inspire people to spend more time in the kitchen.

Always hungry!

 @laurent.dagenais   @laurent.dagenais